GLOBETROTTER™

Travel Guide

P9-CAM-571

CROATIA

ROBIN AND JENNY McKELVIE

NEW HOLLAND

NEW
HOLLAND

★★★ Highly recommended
★★ Recommended
★ See if you can

First edition published in 2006
by New Holland Publishers (UK) Ltd
London • Cape Town • Sydney • Auckland
10 9 8 7 6 5 4 3 2

website: www.newhollandpublishers.com

Garfield House, 86 Edgware Road
London W2 2EA,
United Kingdom

80 McKenzie Street
Cape Town 8001,
South Africa

14 Aquatic Drive,
Frenchs Forest, NSW 2086,
Australia

218 Lake Road,
Northcote, Auckland,
New Zealand

Distributed in the USA by
The Globe Pequot Press, Connecticut

Cover: *A view of Dubrovnik's Old Town.*
Title page: *Varaždin in the hilly region of Zagorje.*

Although every effort has been made to ensure that this
guide is up to date and current at time of going to print,
the Publisher accepts no responsibility or liability for any
loss, injury or inconvenience incurred by readers
or travellers using this guide.

Publishing Manager: Thea Grobbelaar
DTP Cartographic Manager: Genené Hart
Editor: Thea Grobbelaar
Design and DTP: Nicole Bannister
Cartographer: Nicole Bannister
Picture Researcher: Shavonne Johannes
Proofreader and Indexer: Claudia Dos Santos

Reproduction by Resolution, Cape Town
Printed and bound by Times Offset (M) Sdn. Bhd., Malaysia.

Keep us Current
Information in travel guides is apt to change, which is
why we regularly update our guides. We'd be grateful to
receive feedback if you've noted something we should
include in our updates. If you have new
information, please share it with us by writing to the
Publishing Manager, Globetrotter, at the office nearest
to you (addresses on this page). The most significant contribution to each new edition will receive a free
copy of the updated guide.

ISBN 1 84537 062 7

CONTENTS

1
Introducing Croatia

Croatia is quite simply one of the most attractive and enjoyable countries to visit in Europe. Boasting a coastline that eases down the clean waters of the Adriatic Sea in a flurry of 1185 islands, as well as voluminous and largely unspoilt mountains, sweeping plains that offer excellent wines and towns and cities where it often feels as if the 20th century, never mind the 21st, is yet to arrive, Croatia conjures up an intoxicating cocktail that has helped make this oasis one of Europe's fastest growing holiday destinations.

The **coast** is undoubtedly the shining star with its balmy climate, award-winning clean waters and those myriad **islands**, each with its own attractions, whether it be the walking trails and secluded bays of the perfectly preserved green isle of Mljet, or the lavender-scented decadence of Hvar. Part of the attraction is that much of the coastline has only undergone modest development since World War II, unlike other Mediterranean destinations such as Greece and Spain. When the Croatian Tourist Board gushes that this is the 'Mediterranean as it Once Was', they have a point.

But Croatia has much more to offer than its famed coast: inland there is plenty to explore too. The capital, **Zagreb**, is a grand metropolis of one million with all the modern trappings, a rambling Old Town and plenty of green space, as well as numerous day-trip options. To the north are the rolling green hills, health spas and castles of the Zagorje, a land wrapped in legends of ancient knights and defiant partisans.

Opposite: *The southern Dalmatian coast.*

FACT FILE

Croatia's **landmass** is 56,538 km² (21,823 sq miles).
Location: Croatia shares land borders with Hungary, Bosnia-Herzegovina, Serbia and Montenegro and Slovenia. Croatia's Adriatic coast lies to the east of Italy.
Coastline: Croatia has 5835 km (626 miles) of coastline including 1185 **islands**.
Highest mountain: Dinara at 1831m (6008ft) above sea level
Language: Croatian
Population: 4,800,000
Main Religion: Roman Catholic
Government: The HDZ (Croatian Democratic Union) has held office since 2003, under Prime Minister Ivo Sanader.

Break east and **Slavonia** has castles, vineyards and nature reserves. Osijek and Vukovar are settlements that were badly hit by the bitter war of independence during the 1990s. Most of the war damage around Croatia, though, has now been patched up and few visitors notice any sign of the fighting in a country that is now completely safe to visit, and indeed has lower levels of crime than the likes of the UK or France.

Croatia may be relatively unspoilt but this does not mean that it is not adept at looking after visitors, and the north-coast region of **Istria** boasts well-developed package-orientated resorts to back-up its historic towns and Roman architecture. Inland Istria meanwhile is more rural, with small farms and cottages on hand for those wanting to explore a bucolic paradise of vineyards, pretty hill towns and truffles, often deservedly dubbed the 'New Tuscany'.

Further south down the coast the **Kvarner Gulf** is home to a sprinkling of worthwhile islands like Rab and Pag, the elegant Opatija Riviera with its 19th-century hotels and the busy port city of Rijeka. Even further south the long sweep of **Dalmatia** emerges as many people's favourite region. Split is the country's bustling second city, with its old core built around a Roman palace, while in the extreme south **Dubrovnik** is one of Europe's most stunning cities, eulogized by the poet Byron as the 'Pearl of the Adriatic.' There are enough islands in Dalmatia to keep you exploring for months.

Although Croatia more than caters for those looking for a week or two by the sea in the sun, it also increasingly caters for those seeking a more active break. The countryside offers myriad cycling and walking trails, as well as serious mountaineering. Water-based activities include windsurfing, scuba diving and, of course, sailing. Croatia is one of Europe's finest sailing destinations with plenty of marinas and islands on hand up and down the coast.

Whichever part of Croatia you visit, especially if you opt to travel around as much as possible, you can meet the local **people** who actually justify the 'friendly locals' clichés, delve through layers of history with everything from prehistoric sites to Roman remains, and feast on first-rate food. Inland there are hearty soups and spicy meat dishes, while on the coast seafood rules supreme with huge oysters, lobster and a variety of fresh fish appearing on restaurant menus. It is a sign of the quality of food in a country where organic food is the norm that Italian gastronomes now

flock across the Adriatic to enjoy top-notch seafood. Croatian wines also excel with quality white and reds both available.

Whatever you choose to do in Croatia, whether it be cruising around a string of uninhabited islands on a yacht, lotus eating on a beach for a week, or maybe bursting inland to climb a vertiginous mountain peak or rush down a river on a raft, few visitors leave disappointed. In an era of hype and style over substance Croatia actually lives up to all the hyperbole.

Above: *A yacht cruising the Croatian coast.*
Opposite: *Inland Istria, the 'New Tuscany'.*

THE LAND

Croatia is a horseshoe-shaped country that curls around Bosnia-Herzegovina and borders the Republic of Serbia and Montenegro at its northeastern extremity. The northern territory borders Slovenia in the northwest and Hungary in the northeast. A second border with Serbia and Montenegro lies at the southeastern corner. In the west it is fringed by the Adriatic.

Strictly speaking, Croatia is divided into 20 *županje* (administrative counties). However, in practice, Croats often talk about the traditional regions of Dalmatia, Slavonia, Istria and the Kvarner Gulf, regarding the capital Zagreb as a region in itself. Covering some 56,538 km² (21,823 sq miles), Croatia is on a par, in terms of

CLIMATE

The climate in the Croatian hinterland is noticeably different to that on the coast. **Inland** summers can get surprisingly hot, while winters are bitterly cold; the spring is also mild, but autumn can be cold. In contrast the **Croatian Adriatic** basks in a sunny Mediterranean climate with hot summer days and mild winters. Croatia's **hinterland** may be below freezing in January, but winter temperatures on the **coast** range from 5–10°C (40–50°F).

its landmass, with Ireland. For a small country Croatia has a surprisingly diverse geology: fertile valleys, boggy plains, a lengthy coastline and the Dinaric Alps that run along the spine of the country, separating it from Bosnia-Herzegovina.

In the northwest the **Istrian Peninsula** juts out from the mainland, with neighbouring Slovenia staking claim to a small portion of the land in the north. Away from the coast Istria's landscape is one of rolling hills. The eastern part of the peninsula marks the beginning of the **Kvarner Gulf**, with its archipelago of islands, and a coastline flanked by the mountains of Gorski Kotar, Velika Kapela, Mala Kapela and the northern Velebit.

Continuing south to **Dalmatia** the landscape is a combination of hills and mountains, with the Velebit continuing down to Šibenik, from where the Dinaric Alps extend to the Biokovo mountain range that runs behind the Makarska Riviera. Parallel to the Dalmatian mainland, the turquoise Adriatic coast is studded with islands. As Dalmatia extends southwards, the territory occupied by Croatia gets increasingly narrow – en route to Dubrovnik the main highway even passes through Bosnia-Herzegovina at one point.

The bulk of Croatia's landmass is its **hinterland**, with the capital, **Zagreb**, occupying a north central location. Around Zagreb the landscape is mainly hilly, with the Samobor Hills to the west and the Zagorje to the north and northwest. East from Zagreb the scenery changes markedly, giving way to the fertile plains of **Slavonia**, a region traditionally given over to farming. It is here that the marshlands of **Lonjsko Polje Nature Park** (*see* page 52) and **Kopački Rit** (*see* page 66) are located.

With 5835km (3626 miles) of coastline, 4058km (2253 miles) of which fringes the offshore islands, the **Adriatic Sea** is integral to life in Croatia and is home to myriad varieties of marine life from seahorses to dolphins. Seafood dominates in coastal restaurants. Of Croatia's 1185 **islands**, just 50 are inhabited, with a significant number of these accessible by scheduled passenger ferry. Croatia's largest island is Krk (linked to the mainland by the Krk Bridge), followed by Cres, and then the island of Brač. These three hint at the diversity among the islands, with Cres home to a colony of griffon vultures, Krk renowned for its high-quality white wines and the dramatic landscapes of Brač laced with hard rock and infertile soil.

Today **tourism** is the mainstay of Croatia's inhabited islands, with high levels of unemployment outside the tourist season and the isolated location of some resulting in a declining population, although second homeowners have begun to move in and bolster numbers. Even on Brač, just a short ferry ride away from Split, the inhabitants have, in general, emigrated to more hospitable lands choosing to take their trade, often wine making, with them to places like California and Argentina. Yet Croatia's beautiful islands have an irresistible lure and in the years following independence in the 1990s many of the émigrés returned, while some of those who didn't still dream of being buried near their ancestors.

Above: *The Croatian flag flutters above a tour boat en route to the island of Mljet.*

The Kornati Islands are perhaps the most unique. This largely uninhabited archipelago anchored to the west of Zadar and Šibenik is notable for its bareness and harsh conditions; no trees grow on the Kornati Islands nor is there a source of fresh water.

While Croatia's tourist industry focuses firmly on the coast, the country's **lakes** and **rivers** are often overlooked. Croatia's rivers include the Sava, which flows through Zagreb from Slovenia before continuing eastward past Slavonski Brod and into Bosnia-Herzegovina, and the Drava which crosses from the Slovene Border near Varaždin and flows southeast to Osijek and Vukovar in eastern Slavonia before joining the Danube. Shorter, but more well known within tourist circles are the River Krka in northern Dalmatia, with its stunning string of waterfalls and ravines, and the River Cetina

---

MARSHALL TITO

Born Josip Broz in 1892, Tito became a dedicated communist, serving a six-year jail sentence for his beliefs before heading the Partisan resistance movement, who fought against Nazi occupation, the Četniks and the Ustaše (see page 15), during World War II. Tito lead the socialist state of Yugoslavia from the end of the war until his death in 1980. The sirens that rang out on his death also heralded the beginning of the end for the state that he had held together for four decades.

(a favourite spot with white water rafters) that flows into the Adriatic at the central Dalmatian town of Omiš. The Kupa, Dobra, Mrežnica, Korana, Una and Zrmanja rivers are also popular with watersport enthusiasts. Croatia's most famous lakes, the Plitvička Jezera (Plitvice Lakes), are UNESCO World Heritage listed as the **Plitvice Lakes National Park**, and boast natural dams, emerald lakes and powerful waterfalls.

Given its diverse natural make-up it is not surprising that Croatia has two distinct **climatic zone**s, with its coastline basking in a glorious Mediterranean climate where dry, sunny days and balmy temperatures predominate. While summer temperatures in the Croatian hinterland, where there is a continental climate, are also pleasant, the picture is quite different in autumn and winter when the mercury plummets and snow often sets in. The lofty peaks of Croatia's mountains experience their own climate, with alpine conditions such as cool temperatures year-round, and heavy snowfall in winter.

Croatia's craggy mountains, lush plains and marshes provide the habitat for thousands of plant species. **Paklenica National Park** (a UNESCO World Biosphere Reserve) is home to over 2500 varieties of plant life alone. Around the country 18 parks are designated as conservation areas – as either nature reserves or national parks – with a sizable number of birds and wild animals protected under Croatian law. Commonly spotted birds include vultures, falcons, eagles, heron, egrets, cormorants, storks and water fowl.

Wild boar, deer, roebuck, foxes, bears and wolves are just some examples of the wildlife that inhabits Croatia's unspoilt countryside.

Below: *Plitvice Lakes National Park: a UNESCO World Heritage Site.*

HISTORY IN BRIEF
Early History

Little is known about Croatia prior to the arrival of the Romans, who began to settle in the region during the 3rd century BC; but there is some evidence of human settlement dating back to the **Stone Age**. By the 4th century BC the Greeks had begun to make parts of the Dalmatian coastline their home, living side by side with the Illyrian tribes.

Romans

Roman settlement in Croatia was a gradual process that began some time during the 3rd century BC, when the Greeks, who were concerned about the southeasterly expansion of the Illyrian tribes, sought military assistance. By the 1st century BC the Romans had broken up the Illyrian threat and gained control over much of present-day Croatia, splitting the country into two provinces: Dalmatia in the south and Pannier (including parts of modern-day Slovenia) in the north.

Croatia's Roman heritage is still on display along the coast, with extensive **Roman remains** to be found at Salona (near Solin on the fringes of Split), Split itself, Trogir, Poreč, Zadar and Pula. The two-stage collapse of the Roman Empire – with the Eastern part falling in AD365 and the Western part in 476 – heralded the end of Croatia's Roman era. The most famous Roman in Croatia's history was the **Emperor Diocletian**, who rose to power in AD284 and ordered the construction of his retirement palace on the central Dalmatian coast. Diocletian's Palace is still standing today in Split, the region's capital.

Slavs/Croats

Historians are a bit hazy about when exactly the first 'Croats' arrived in Croatia, but there is a broad consensus that Slavic tribes began to migrate south from modern-day Poland at the beginning of the 7th century,

Above: *A display in Zagreb's Ethnographic Museum.*

POLITICAL FOOTBALLS

The passionate fans of **Dinamo Zagreb** (the 'Blue Boys') and **Hadjuk Split** (the Torcida) have blurred the line between sport and politics. The Blue Boys fought against Tudman's nationalist revamp of their club as Croatia Zagreb and actually defeated him in a major blow to a government that eventually fell. In the south, in Split, the Torcida for decades fought their own battles with the Serb-dominated police and authorities (some fans were actually jailed) and today they stand up against the political dominance of Zagreb through the forum of football.

FOOTBALL

Coming third in the Football World Cup in France in 1998 was quite some achievement for a country that had only been independent since 1991. With so little political punch many Croats see sport as a way of putting the country on the map and their heroes have responded by qualifying for both World Cups and European Championships as well as beating bitter rival neighbours Italy and Slovenia. Croatia always provided its fair share of players for the Yugoslav national team before 1991 and these days many of its players have contracts with big clubs in Italy and Spain.

Below: *Statue of King Tomislav in Zagreb.*

and that they became the dominant people in modern-day Croatia by the end of that century. The notion of a separate Croatian identity really began to take shape in 879 when Rome bestowed the status of an independent state, under Branimir, on Croatia.

Tomislav and the First Croat Kingdom

The Croatian Duke Tomislav, who governed Croatia from 910–928, increased the status and power of the Croatian state when he commanded an army which defeated forces from Bulgaria and Hungary; victories that saw the country's territory include the northwestern part of modern-day Bosnia-Herzegovina and more northerly regions of present-day Croatia. As a reward for his military prowess, Tomislav was crowned the **first Croatian king** by Pope Clement IV in 925.

Austro-Hungarians

King Zvonimir, who died in 1089, was the last of Croatia's kings, with an already changing balance of power in Croatia sealed by the country's union with Hungary in 1102 under the Pacta Conventa. This pact saw Croatia pledge its allegiance to the Hungarian king, **Koloman**, while retaining the status of an independent state with its own parliament and Ban (the viceroy, appointed to take charge of the country on behalf of the monarch). Croatia's most famous Ban was **Josip Jelačić** (1801–59) who took on the role in 1848 at a time of political unrest and calls for greater independence from Hungary. Jelačić was a fervent Croatian patriot and his most popular acts included the overhaul of the feudal system and the active pursuit of Croatian independence from Hungary, which saw him declare war on the Hungarian state in the same year as his election.

Venetian Influence

Political union with Hungary was to shape the daily life of Croats in the country's hinterland over the next four centuries, but for those on the coast the picture was quite different. Here the beginning of the 12th century marked the start of Venice's powerful influence. By a combination of military strikes and land purchases, the Divine Republic gained control over the majority of Dalmatia and parts of Istria over the next two centuries.

Above: *The crest of the powerful Habsburgs.*

Habsburgs and the Ottoman Threat

Venice and Hungary were not the only foreign powers to take a role in Croatian history, and by the 14th century the Ottoman Empire had also become a significant player, threatening Hungarian dominance inland in particular. By 1526 the Ottoman Turks had won control over much of the Croatian territory formerly ruled by Hungary. The crowning of Austria's **King Ferdinand** in 1527 was one step taken to redress the balance of power in the region, as it incorporated Hungary and those parts of the Croatian state still unified with it into the Habsburg Empire – a move that marked the beginning of a period of Austro-Hungarian dominion that lasted almost 400 years.

Despite the heightened power of the Austro-Hungarian Empire, the Ottomans remained a powerful force and the tussle for control over Croatian territory continued until the 17th century, when a series of Austrian victories that began in the previous century left Austria-Hungary firmly in control.

Illyrian Provinces

When **Napoleon Bonaparte** seized control of Venice in 1797, the Dalmatian coast, part of the Venetian Empire at the time, briefly became part of the French emperor's

CHILDREN'S CROATIA

Croatia's main attraction for children are the beaches; however, most lack the one thing that many people expect from a beach-based holiday – sand. Instead, shingle and even concrete platforms are more usual. Compensating for this, many resort beaches have water-slides, banana boats and other water sports. Family orientated hotels frequently have sports complexes, as do larger camp sites. Children are welcome almost everywhere in Croatia, with discounts given for food, travel and lodgings.

DISABLED TRAVELLERS

One of Croatia's great charms is its numerous old towns with their warrens of narrow, cobbled streets; unfortunately this can make access more difficult for anyone using a wheelchair. The majority of hotels in these historic cores do not have lifts, with bedrooms situated on the upper floors. Some modern hotels do have rooms modified for disabled visitors, rooms located on the ground floor, or guest lifts. Travellers with disabilities should contact a tourist office for advice.

Illyrian Provinces before being subsumed into the Austro-Hungarian Empire at the Congress of Vienna in 1815. Political wrangling at the congress gave the Austro-Hungarian coalition control over Croatia. When the alliance disintegrated in 1867 Croatia was divided again, with the hinterland becoming part of Hungary's territory and Dalmatia going to the Austrians.

World War I

The next defining event in Croatia's history came in 1914 when, in a prelude to World War I, the Archduke Ferdinand was assassinated in nearby Sarajevo. As tensions in Europe spilled over into all-out war, Croatia entered the fray on the side of Austria-Hungary. The four-year conflict sounded the death knell for the Austro-Hungarian Empire and Croatia entered the next phase of its history as a member of the Kingdom of Serbs, Croats and Slovenes.

Kingdom of Serbs, Croats and Slovenes

Below: *A 'Welcome to Croatia' sign on the island of Korčula.*

Croatia's union with Serbia and Slovenia was difficult right from the start with Croat sensibilities stirred by the 1921 **Vidovdan Constitution**, which formally centred power in Serbia. The murder of Stjepan Radić, the leader of the Croatian Peasants' Party, by a Serbian radical, Puniša Racić, in 1928 and the institution of a royal dictatorship, under the Serbian **King Alexander**, in 1929 added still more fuel to the Croats' desire for independence.

In 1934 King Alexander was assassinated. The Croatian Ustaše, a hard-line fascist movement, was implicated in his murder. The fascists were not the only people pushing for a change in the Kingdom of Serbs, Croats and Slovenes at this time – pressure was also being exerted by Tito's Communist Party. Croatia was granted an untimely autonomy within Yugoslavia, on the eve of the World War II in 1939.

World War II

By 1941 the Kingdom of Serbs, Croats and Slovenes had become embroiled in World War II and the split in the country's allegiances highlighted the deep divisions that existed within the fragile kingdom. Those loyal to Tito and the Communist Party took up arms alongside the partisan resistance fighters who fought against the Nazi forces and the Ustaše (see panel, page 53). The Ustaše, led by Ante Pavalić, gave their support to Hitler, a move that saw the emergence of a Nazi puppet state in the guise of the **Independent State of Croatia** (NDH) in 1941. Another group of extreme paramilitaries were the Četniks. This radical group was comprised mainly of Serbs who fought against occupying forces, and for a time enjoyed support from the Allies.

Tito's Yugoslavia

As World War II neared its climax the Allied forces switched allegiance and gave their support to the Partisans, backing Tito as the leader of the new state of Yugoslavia in 1945. At the end of the war, thousands of fleeing Ustaše were sent back into Yugoslavia, where they were executed at the hands of the Partisans after having been handed over by British forces. Tito himself was implicated in this atrocity, but his direct involvement has never been proven. The new Yugoslavian leader's next move was to reject overtures made by **Stalin** for a close alignment with Soviet Russia. The new federation, comprised of Serbs, Croats, Slovenes, Macedonians, Bosnians and Montenegrins, soon proved almost as fragile as the inter-war unison, and once again Croats began to resent the dominance of the Serbs.

The 1966 Croatian Spring was an expression of Croatian nationalism within Yugoslavia as resentment grew. Similar to the Prague Spring, this was a flowering of Croatian culture and was supported by Tito in its early stages. As the potential threat of Serbian dominance and a Yugoslav state became apparent, Tito quickly changed his mind and ordered a clampdown on the main protagonists. In Croatia the publication in

Above: A statue of Tito on the island of Vis.

Above: *A Croatian flag in the capital city of Zagreb.*

the early 1970s of the first Serbo-Croat dictionary, in which Croatian appeared to be a lesser language, also stimulated the fermenting desire for independence.

Disintegration of Yugoslavia

After 37 years of rule, Tito's death in 1980 was effectively the beginning of the end for Yugoslavia. His strong personal belief in a unified Yugoslavia with a shared national identity had managed to meld the six distinct republics together for almost four decades, yet when he passed away there was no clear successor or way forward. The next 10 years were marked by growing discontent from all over the federation, particularly from within Croatia and Slovenia, who believed that their stronger economies were being used to subsidize the rest of Yugoslavia. This decade also saw the emergence of increasingly pro-Serb policies and a greater centralization of power in Belgrade. **Slobodan Milosevic**, who came to power in 1989, stirred up ethnic and religious tensions and promised the Serbian people that they would continue to enjoy superiority in Yugoslavia.

Croatian War of Independence

By 1991 the vast majority of Croats believed that their position within Yugoslavia was untenable and in June the Croatian parliament declared the country independent, echoing the mood of the people who had overwhelmingly voted for independence in the May referendum. This move was swiftly followed by the eruption of fighting as the **Yugoslav National Army** (JNA) moved in, supposedly to separate the Croats and the rebel Serbs in the east and centre of Croatia, though in reality they sided with the Serbs.

The most ferocious fighting tore through the country between 1991 and the end of 1992 as the Serbs added a sickening new word to the global lexicon: 'ethnic cleansing'; whole areas were cleared of Croats by the Serbs (backed up by the might of the 'neutral' army). The war saw Serb irregulars turn on their neighbours, murdering villagers and burying them in mass graves like that in Ovčara, just outside Vukovar. The eastern province of Slavonia was the worst hit; the riverside town of Vukovar was decimated. By 1993 a UN-brokered ceasefire was holding, and Croatian offensives later the same year and in 1995 won back most of the territory captured, the remainder following under UN supervision in 1998.

Twenty-first Century Croatia

By 1998 all Croatian land had been returned and the country's tourist industry, particularly along the coast, was well on its way to recovery after a half decade of turbulence. Today Croatia is a safe destination to visit, with no specific safety concerns. Resentment continues between some Serbs who stayed behind after the war and returning Croats, but this very rarely impacts on any visitors, though you should be sensitive when discussing the war and regional political issues.

The Independent Republic of Dubrovnik

Dubrovnik has a history distinct from the rest of Croatia. The first settlers arrived in the city-state during the 7th century AD, and established Ragusa on the small island of Lausa (from which it derived its Latin name). Later, the narrow channel separating Ragusa from the new territory of Dubrovnik, located at the base of Mount Srd, was filled in (today this is the Stradun) and the city of Dubrovnik was created.

Until 1205 Byzantine rulers protected the city, after which time it fell into the hands of Venice. In 1358 control of

---

FESTIVAL SEASON

From June to August festivals of classical, folk and contemporary music, theatre, dance and art take place all over Croatia. Street entertainment and carnival processions are also inherent to the festivals. The Kvarner Gulf islands of Rab, Krk and Pag, and the Dalmatian island of Korčula are among the most atmospheric performance venues. On the mainland, the Basilica of Euphrasius in Poreč and Pula's Roman Amphitheatre also provide a stage for unforgettable productions.

Below: *War cemetery on the outskirts of Vukovar.*

PRIVATE ACCOMMODATION

Demand for accommodation in Croatia's coastal towns is high, with hotel capacity woefully inadequate during the peak season. Many tourists choose instead to rent rooms (*sobe*) or private apartments. These are relatively cheap and can be arranged at travel agents operating in key tourist areas. If you are intending to stay for less than three days you will generally have to pay a 30% surcharge, and some owners may even refuse to take you.

Dubrovnik changed hands again and it became part of the Hungarian-Croatian Kingdom, an event that propelled the city towards economic prosperity.

Under Hungarian rule Dubrovnik was granted the status of an independent city-state and rapidly extended its influence over Lastovo, which became part of the Independent Republic of Dubrovnik's territory during the 13th century, and the Pelješac Peninsula and the island of Mljet in the 14th century. By this time the republic's land extended from the walled town of Ston in the north to present-day Cavtat which is located at Croatia's southern tip.

By the 16th century, Dubrovnik had solidified its position as the most powerful economic centre on the eastern Adriatic coast, and it had also become a place of scientific and literary development, and gradually extended its diplomatic presence throughout the Mediterranean. In addition to its economic prosperity, Dubrovnik also had a substantial navy, its growing fleet of ships (thought to have been 300 strong by the 18th century) posing a major threat to the might of the Venetian Republic. The rockiest period during these three centuries was the 1667 earthquake, which razed most of the city's buildings and also weakened its power during the lengthy rebuilding process.

Napoleon Bonaparte's early 19th-century incursions effectively ended the republic's long period of self-rule, with Napoleonic forces taking control of the city in 1806. By 1808 the Independent Republic of Dubrovnik had been abolished and incorporated into Napoleon's Illyrian provinces. Once Napoleon was defeated, Dubrovnik became part of the Austro-Hungarian Empire as a result of the 1815 Congress of Vienna.

Below: *The scars of war on a bridge in Dubrovnik.*

Another leadership change came for Dubrovnik's inhabitants in 1920 as the city was subsumed into the newly created Kingdom of Serbs, Croats and Slovenes. During World War II Dubrovnik was occupied by Nazi troops, emerging from the conflict as part of Yugoslavia.

The next defining moment in the city's history came in 1991 when it was shelled as part of the Serb offensive during Croatia's war of independence. The shells that fell on the UNESCO World Heritage city in 1991 and 1992 brought the conflict to the world's attention and saw swathes of buildings in the historic core damaged. Fortunately most of the damage was quickly repaired and today Dubrovnik has re-established itself as a key tourist destination.

Above: *The bustling streets of 21st-century Zagreb.*

GOVERNMENT AND ECONOMY
The Constitution

Croatia is a republic with a democratic system of government and separate legislative and executive bodies. Decisions about the day-to-day running of the country are made in the **Hrvatski Sabor** (Croatian Parliament), whose 152 members are elected by a secret public ballot that takes place every four years. When Croatia declared its independence in 1991, **Franjo Tuđman** emerged as the country's first president; yet he and his political party, the HDZ (Croatian Democratic Union), were soon surrounded by controversy and claims that he afforded his advisers, and friends, more power than the Sabor. Since Tuđman's death in 1999 and the first democratic election of a Croatian president, this balance of power has been redressed. The election, in January 2000, of Prime Minister **Ivica Račan** at the helm of a coalition between the SDP (Social Democratic Party) and the HSLS (Croatian Social Liberal Party) was also seen as an expression of dissatisfaction with the HDZ. To the surprise of some political observers the HDZ were returned to power in

---

CROATIAN SPIRITS

Some Croats will happily confess that Croats enjoy their alcohol, saying 'If drinking before midday means we have a drinking problem, then all Croats are alcoholics.' This may be an exaggeration, but many do have a penchant for fiery spirits like *šljivovica*, a plum brandy originating in Eastern Croatia, *travarica*, a herb brandy, and the grape-based grappa. The latter often appears as a complimentary digestive and can be hard to refuse when offered by friendly and insistent locals.

December 2003, with **Ivo Sanader** the country's current Prime Minister. Presidential elections in Croatia are held every five years and **Stipe Mešic**, Tuđman's successor, won a second term in office by a comfortable majority in January 2005.

Economic Patterns

As part of Yugoslavia, Croatia had a strong economy that thrived on industry and, along the coast, tourism. Compared to the other Yugoslav republics Croatia punched above its weight in economic terms and generated around a third of the country's GDP (Gross Domestic Product). Growing dissatisfaction with money being siphoned off to Belgrade is one of the reasons that Croats came out and voted overwhelmingly for independence in 1991.

Collateral damage sustained as a result of a four-year war (although much of the fighting actually ended in 1992), political instability in the Balkan region (which perpetuated the mistaken belief that Croatia was not a safe place to visit), a substantial foreign debt and, in the early 1990s, a large number of displaced refugees, saw the economy of the newly independent country flounder. The collapse of its trading links within the former Yugoslavia compounded these difficulties.

Today Croatia has a much stronger and more stable economy (as witnessed by its recent negotiations to become part of the European Union), with clearly visible evidence of national and international investment taking the form of myriad reconstruction and renovation projects throughout the country.

Below: *The busy loading docks at Pula.*

It is not just Croatia's construction industry that is booming: telecommunications, utilities and tourism also generate considerable revenues. Statistics published by the Croatian Tourist Board suggest that the number of tourists who visit Croatia each year now exceeds pre-1991 levels.

Infrastructure

Prior to 1991, as part of a deliberate Yugoslav policy, few direct motorways or railways were built between Croatia's cities, with all main routes leading to Belgrade instead. This made travelling around Croatia a frustrating experience, as the railways were outdated and slow and necessitated circuitous and time-consuming connections. Roads were little better, the majority comprising a single lane in each direction, including the greater part of the main coastal road, the Jadranska Magistrala (Adriatic Highway), which links Rijeka in the north with Dubrovnik in the south.

Above: *A train in Pula.*

A lot has been done recently to improve Croatia's transport infrastructure, with the efficient national airline, Croatia Airlines, reducing fares on domestic flights, and the construction of new motorways between Zagreb and Rijeka and Zagreb and Split. Investment in Croatia's railways has proved more troublesome. In the summer of 2004 a new express service began operating between Zagreb and Split, reducing the journey time by two and a half hours to five hours. After operating throughout the peak tourist months the train was withdrawn from service for essential track maintenance. There are suggestions that it may not reopen until at least 2007.

Croatia and the European Union

Some observers predict that Croatia will join the European Union (EU) as early as 2008 and at the beginning of the 21st century the majority of Croats appeared to support the idea of membership. However, the re-election of the HDZ in 2003 was just one indication of resistance to EU hegemony. Dissatisfaction with the policies of the HDZ in the early years of independence saw them ousted from power in 2000, only to return four years later. In the interim Račan's coalition party

BEST BUYS

Traditional Croatian handicrafts make great keepsakes and gifts. These tend to vary according to region, and highlights include Pag lace and cheese, Istrian truffles, Hvar lavender and *morčić* jewellery from Rijeka. Elegant glassware, good quality silver jewellery and items made from Adriatic coral are sold in tourist shops throughout Dalmatia. Universal souvenirs include embroidery, dolls and sculptures wearing traditional costumes, ceramics, wooden handicrafts and ties, as well as Croatian wine, herb brandy and olive oil.

AT THE MARKET

Bustling markets are commonplace in towns and cities throughout Croatia. In Zagreb the *Dolac* (see page 40), held in the shadow of the cathedral, is a place to buy foodstuffs, honey, football memorabilia and traditional souvenirs. Fresh fruit and vegetables are sold each morning in the heart of Dubrovnik's Old Town, with a similar market operating by the ferry terminal. In Split and Trogir the markets sit just outside the respective old towns.

had been cooperating with The Hague and surrendered Croatian generals, widely considered as heroes within Croatia, to war criminal tribunals. It has been suggested that this is one of the main reasons that Račan's SDP and HSLS alliance fell out of favour. Any future refusal to hand over indicted Croats could well block the process of joining the EU.

Many of the Croats who have been keeping a keen eye on the EU also look to Germany as a measure of its success, regarding a struggling economy, and media reports that lay the blame at the door of immigrant workers, as evidence against membership. These anxieties work on two levels, with some fearing that the prospect of earning more money in other EU countries will see a mass exodus of Croatian talent, while others worry that foreigners will come to Croatia seeking work in an economy where unemployment regularly runs up to 15%.

THE PEOPLE
Ethnic and Religious Mix
Croatia's 4.8 million population is relatively homogenous. The country's biggest ethnic groups are Croatian (90%), Serbian (4%), Bosnian (0.5%) and Hungarian (0.5%). Despite this ethnic majority, Croats come from diverse backgrounds, with those living on the coast being the ancestors of the Greeks and Venetians (see pages 11–13). Meanwhile Croats living in the hinterland, particularly in Slavonia in the east, often come from marriages between Croats, Hungarians, Germans, Slovaks, and Czechs. Intermarriage between Serbs, Slovenes, Croats, Bosnians, Macedonians and Montenegrins was common during the 20th century and continues to this day.

Traditional Cultures
It is not just parentage that distinguishes those living in the Croatian hinterland from the coastal inhabitants. Life inland has been shaped by centuries of Austro-Hungarian dominance, but daily living along the coast

has a distinctly Italian feel. As a result these regions differ on almost every level including cuisine, architecture, customs and cultures. Croats living along the coast even often look different to those hailing from the central and eastern parts of Croatia; the former are tall and dark, while the latter tend to be shorter and fairer haired.

Traditional customs are kept alive in the many folk festivals that crowd the Croatian calendar. Meanwhile in towns across Croatia different events and rituals are re-enacted during Carnival. More contemporary and classical culture comes to the fore in the myriad summer festivals.

Above: *Lively traditional dancing in Dubrovnik's Old Town.*

Food and drink

Cold winters and fertile plains, ideal for animal farming, have resulted in a tradition of dining on hearty meat dishes and stodgy strudels in hinterland homes, while mild coastal temperatures and an abundance of fresh fish have seen the diet along the Adriatic dominated by the daily catch, with the likes of John Dory, sea bass, sole, lobster, scampi, mussels and clams readily available. Domestically and commercially produced alcohol has long been part of Croatian life, yet even this differs between the coast (*primorska*) and the plains (*panonia*). It is estimated that around 70% of all the wine produced in Croatia is white, with a geographical split between colours – 90% of wines from the hinterland are white, while 70% of the wines produced on the coast are red.

Inland the most common varieties of white grape are Grasevina, Riesling and Chardonnay, with Sauvignon and Frankovka being the most popular reds in this area.

BASIC MANNERS

Requests should always be followed with a 'please' and a 'thank you' given for service. Croatians also consider it polite to say hello and goodbye to people. Any attempt to speak Croatian is genuinely appreciated and may solicit comments about how good your Croatian is, without any hint of sarcasm. Key phrases are:
Dobar Dan – good day
Molim – please
Hvala – thank you
Do videnja – goodbye

Above: *Ripening vines in Croatia.*

Along the coast the red Plavac, Postup and Dingač grapes dominate, with some wineries trying their hand at the production of Merlot and Cabernet Sauvignon in more recent years. Quality white wines grown in the coastal regions include Malvasia, Debit, Pošip and Zlahtina. Domestic spirits consumed in Croatia include *šljivovica* (plum brandy), *travarica* (herb brandy), grappa (grape brandy) and maraschino (sour cherry liqueur).

Daily Life

The majority of Croatians, especially the younger generation, are highly educated and driven individuals who, while they may take their inspiration from the past, look firmly towards the future and are working very hard to build a stronger, more confident Croatia. On the whole, Croatians are warm, welcoming and courteous. Despite these shared characteristics, Croats living on the coast, especially in Dalmatia, tend to exhibit very different attitudes to their hinterland counterparts. Recreation, fashion, romance, literature and art are all considered important by twenty- and thirtysomething Dalmatians, while inland pragmatism is an inherent aspect of daily life.

For those Croats living in Slavonia it is even harder to share the Dalmatians' positive outlook, as the local economy remains depressed and the scars of war all too visible. The emotional wounds in this part of the country are still raw, with Serbs and Croats sharing the town of Vukovar (*see page 63*), but living in a way that could hardly be described as side-by-side.

Croatian Nationalism

Croats share a strong national identity, and pride in their language and folkloric traditions has risen from centuries of suppression by foreign rulers. Nationalism

CROATIAN WINE

The quality of Croatian wine is one of the most pleasant surprises for many visitors to the country. Production is relatively small scale, often family run. Cheap and cheerful table wine like Plavac is widely available; however, connoisseurs should try the red Dingač and Postup, or the white Pošip, Vrbnička Žlahtina and Graševina. You can also pop into one of the many wine cellars (*kleti*) that you will find around the country.

was also intensified by the high cost (both fiscally and in terms of human life) of independence. Today the majority of Croats are proud to be Croatian, with this sentiment frequently expressed through the Catholic faith and the importance placed on religious festivals and pilgrimages.

Sport and Recreation

Fashion, art, literature and politics are not the only things that stir Croats. Croatia is also a nation of sports fans – cheering on the team is another outlet for expressing pride in the country or a home town. Football is the most popular spectator sport, spawning celebrities like Davor Šuker and Robert Jarni (both ex Real Madrid players), Zvonimir Boban (formerly of AC Milan) and Alen Boksic who played for Marseille, Juventus and Lazio. Other Croatian sporting heroes include the tennis players Goran Ivanišević, Ivan Ljubćić, Iva Majoli and Karolina Šprem, the skier Janica Kostelić, as well as NBA basketball players Dražen Petrović and Kresmir Cosic. Tragically, the former died in a car crash in 1993 and the latter succumbed to non-Hodgkins lymphoma in 1995.

Arts

Croatia has a strong arts tradition, its most celebrated luminaries including the 20th-century sculptor Ivan Meštrović, and also those working in the medium of classical, modern and naïve art.

Born in the small Slavonian village of Vrpolje, **Ivan Meštrović** (1883–1962) studied sculpture in Vienna (1901–06) before working and living in Paris, then Zagreb, Split, Rome, Switzerland and the United States, eventu-

> ### DECLINING POPULATION
>
> Despite the existence of a deep-seated national pride the population of Croatia is declining. Graduates are attracted to lucrative salaries offered abroad and there is a trend of delaying parenthood. Many of Croatia's young people, like those from all over Europe, are choosing to have fewer children later in life, giving them more time to travel, socialize and dedicate themselves to the pursuit of the latest fashions.

Below: *Young Croatians celebrating after a football win over Italy.*

EATING TIPS

• Not all restaurants, including some expensive ones, take credit cards.
• The best restaurants are often located away from main tourist areas.
• Restaurants in residential areas are often much cheaper.
• The daily special is generally the freshest and most affordable option.
Useful phrases:
Molim vas jelovnik? – Can I have the menu?
vinsku kartu – wine list
Bilo je jako dobro – It was delicious
Račun molim – The bill please

Opposite: *An art gallery in the Istria region.*
Below: *Sculpture of Antun Gustav Matos, Zagreb.*

ally becoming a citizen of the latter. Meštrović cited Michelangelo and Rodin among his influences, and the style of his work changed as he grew older, his earlier sculpture often having religious themes and being carved mainly from wood. He then moved on to more personal pieces that highlighted the frailties of human beings, among them nudes and portraits like the **Woman with Lute**.

Some of Meštrović's most famous outdoor sculptures are on public display in Croatia, including the statue of **Josip Juraj Strossmayer** and the **Well of Life** in Zagreb, and various versions of **Grgur of Nin** that reside in Varaždin, Nin and Split, with the latter nine-metre giant being the biggest and most impressive. Another of Meštrović's most celebrated pieces, **Monument to the Indians**, takes pride of place in Chicago's Central Park. Today the Meštrović Foundation (visit their website at www.mdc.hr) maintains displays of the sculptor's work at various locations: in his former Zagreb home, at the Meštrović Gallery in Split, The Most Holy Redeemer Church in Otavice and The Holy Crucifix Church in Kaštelet-Cirkvine.

Croatia boasts a wealth of artistic talent that spans the centuries: some of the country's most famous **painters** include Julije Klović (1498–1578), whose classical European miniatures are exhibited in some of the most eminent galleries throughout the world, including the Uffizi, the British Museum and the Louvre, and Vlaho Bukovac (1855–1922), renowned for his portraits and who also worked as a professor at Prague's Academy of Art. Highly regarded modern Croatian artists include Slava Raška (1877–1906), Josip Račić (1885–1908), Miroslav Kraljević (1885–1913), Ferdinand Kulmer (b. 1925) and Edo Murlić (b. 1921).

One of Croatia's best-known artistic genres is **naïve art**, a movement that began in the rural village of Hlebine near the country's border with Hungary. Naïve art can best be described as simple, almost innocent paintings, of things important to daily life in the countryside, such as peasant dwellings and folk traditions. This artistic style was fuelled by the 1930s depression, which bought greater poverty and hardship to rural villagers. Ivan Generalić (1914–92) is arguably Croatia's most famous naïve artist, and works by Ivan Rabuzin (b. 1921), Ivan Iacković-Croata (1932– 2004) and Ilija Bosilj-Basicevic (1895– 1972) are also highly regarded.

The last 500 years in the history of **Croatian literature** have been intrinsically tied into the development of **Croatian nationalism** and the Croat identity. The origins of this lie with the renaissance in South Slavic literature that began in the 15th century.

Arguably the most important figure from this era is Marko Marulić (1450–1524), who is commonly heralded as the father of Croatian literature and whose best-known Croatian work is the epic biblical poem *Judita*, which he penned three years before his death. At the beginning of the 16th century the writings of the Hvar-born poets Hanibal Lucić (1485–1553) and Petar Hetorović (1487–1572) rose to the fore, as did the prose and plays of Marin Držić (1508–67) who hailed from from Dubrovnik.

The poet Ivan Gundulić (1588–1638) made a significant contribution to Croatian literature and national identity in the next century. One of Gundulić's most famous offerings was *Osman*, written in 1626, which romanticized the Polish struggles against Turkey, and was regarded as a clear endorsement of the Croatian (Slavic) nationalist cause.

Another significant moment in the development of the Croatian language, within the context of literature, came in 1841 when the Croat poet and politician Ivan

CUISINE

Each region of Croatia has its own culinary traditions, with fresh Adriatic fish dominating menus along the coast and hearty meat dishes predominating inland. In Central and Eastern Croatia look out for, *janje na ražnju* (spit roast lamb) and *pečeni odojak na ražnju* (spit roast suckling pig). Typical Istrian dishes include *tartufi* (truffles) and *pršut* (air-dried ham). Dalmatia also boasts its own version of *pršut*, and the Kvarner Gulf's most famous dishes – *Paški sir* (hard sheep cheese) and *Paški janje* (Pag lamb) – come from Pag.

SIGHTSEEING TIPS

• Get up early to avoid the hordes in the peak season; this is particularly true in Dubrovnik when the cruise ship passengers disembark.
• Check opening hours in advance; many museums are closed on Mondays, and opening hours are curtailed in winter.
• Many tourist offices distribute self-guided walking tours and free maps.
• Make sure you have plenty of fresh drinking water.
• The Croatian sun burns all year, so remember your sunglasses and sunscreen.

Mažuranić (1814–90) jointly wrote the first German to Illyrian (Croatian) dictionary alongside Josip Užarević. In the same century the oratory of the politician and writer Ljudevit Gaj (1809–72) called for the use of Croatian and equality of Croats within the Austro-Hungarian empire. Another key member of the Illyrian movement during the 19th century was August Šenoa (1838–81) who wrote about the oppression of the Croatian peasants and introduced the historical novel to his home country. Nazar Vladimir (1876– 1949) is widely regarded as one of the main propagators of Croatian nationalism during the 20th century, with his poem, *Croat Kings*, regarded as a tool that stirred the Croat national conscience.

Architecture

For many first-time visitors Croatia's diverse architecture and its breathtaking Italianate coastal towns come as a real and very pleasant surprise. The country's architectural diversity is accounted for, at least in part, by its varied history with Roman, Austrian, Hungarian and Italian influences evident in towns and cities throughout. The structures in Zagreb and the Croatian hinterland are heavily influenced by Vienna, with grand neo-Classical buildings (such as the Croatian Parliament or *Sabor*) and neo-Baroque masterpieces (like the Croatian National Theatre) all part of the mix. Some fine examples of Art Nouveau, Baroque and Medieval architecture are also to be found in the capital.

One of the seminal figures in Zagreb's modern-day appearance is architect Herman Bollé (1845–1926) who was responsible for the 19th-century neo-Gothic reconstruction

Below: *Gothic window on the island of Hvar.*

of the cathedral and the renovation of both St Mark's Church and St Catherine's Church.

In the coastal towns of Istria and Dalmatia the predominant style of the architecture is Venetian, with Romanesque cathedrals and Venetian bell towers dominating the skylines.

Assigning a single architectural style to the coast and the hinterland

Above: *The Venetian-era district of Kut on the island of Vis.*

simplifies the picture, as the evolution of Croatia's towns and cities has been influenced by so many different cultures.

Dubrovnik's Baroque Old Town, with its stunning cathedral, the 15th- and 16th-century Renaissance architecture of Šibenik, with its dramatic cathedral (constructed entirely from marble and limestone quarried on the island of Brač), and the Medieval town of Trogir are among some of the country's most impressive set pieces. The churches of St Donat in Zadar and St Kriz in Nin are particularly striking examples of pre-Romanesque or Croatian sacral architecture. Elsewhere, Split's cathedral is an impressive testimony to the Hellenistic style and, in the Istrian city of Poreč, the Basilica of Euphrasius is a masterpiece of Byzantine architecture.

With myriad Gothic chapels and churches, Venetian campaniles and Romanesque spires all part of Croatia's architectural heritage, it is perhaps unsurprising that a number of the country's monuments have found their way onto the UNESCO World Heritage List. The turn of the 20th century bought a new Modernist influence to the country, with examples of Italian Modernism most evident in Zagreb's central Trg Bana Josip Jelačića and the Kvarner Gulf port city of Rijeka.

LANGUAGE

One legacy of a long history of unions and alliances with other nations is the apparent ease with which many Croats seem to master foreign languages. As the language of business, English is widely spoken across the country, although less so among the older residents. Along the coast you are also likely to find Croatians who are fluent in Italian, while those in the hinterland can often speak German. The languages of the former Yugoslav republics are also commonly understood, particularly among the older generation.

2
Zagreb

For a city never designed to be a national capital, Zagreb manages to conjure up an impressive big-city buzz – all rumbling trams, stately façades and rushing commuters. It is an elegant metropolis of one million in the grand *Mitteleuropa* tradition, with many of its lavish buildings and arrow-straight avenues laid out in the 19th century. Since becoming capital of the Republic of Croatia in 1991 Zagreb has enjoyed a new lease on life, and on busy Bana Josip Jelačića Square any anachronistic images of what an 'Eastern European' city should be like are brushed aside by the slick new trams, abundance of glass, steel and neon, and the mêlée of mobile phone-sporting businessmen and art-fully grungy students who make up one of the most youthful populations of any city in Europe.

The centre is divided into the Gornji (upper) and Donji (lower) towns. Take the funicular to **Gornji Grad** where winding cobbled streets reveal the medieval origins of the city's oldest quarter. There are also green lungs to explore. The parks of Maksimir and Jarun, as well as Mount Medvednica, are a real escape for walkers and skiers.

Donji Grad could not be more different. The hub of local life, this grid-like plain with its grand architecture is easily explored on foot as it is pancake flat and there are numerous bars, cafés and restaurants to keep you going along the way. The local tourist office publishes a free map with a numbered walking trail, handy for those short on time, and they can arrange guided tours.

DON'T MISS

*** St Mark's Church: 13th-century Gothic church with a brightly coloured tile roof.
*** Zagreb Cathedral: attractively overhauled by renowned architect Herman Bollé in the 19th century.
*** Atelje Meštrović: an impressive array of the great man's sculptures on display in his stunning former home.
*** Strossmayerovo Šetalište: views of the Donji Grad and the Cathedral.
*** Medvednica: great for walkers, or skiing in winter.
*** The Regent Esplanade Hotel: grand old dame of Orient Express fame.

Opposite: *Trg Bana Josip Jelačića in Zagreb.*

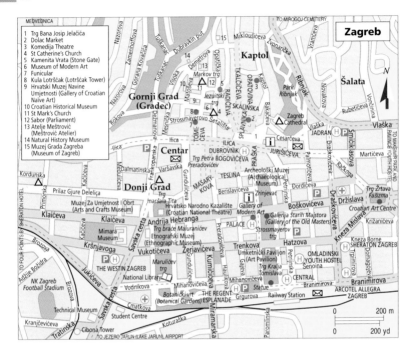

Zagreb

1 Trg Bana Josip Jelačića
2 Dolac Market
3 Komedija Theatre
4 St Catherine's Church
5 Kamenita Vrata (Stone Gate)
6 Museum of Modern Art
7 Funicular
8 Kula Lotrščak (Lotrščak Tower)
9 Hrvatski Muzej Navine
  Umjetnosti (Gallery of Croatian
  Naïve Art)
10 Croatian Historical Museum
11 St Mark's Church
12 Sabor (Parliament)
13 Atelje Meštrović
  (Meštrović Atelier)
14 Natural History Museum
15 Muzej Grada Zagreba
  (Museum of Zagreb)

A TRIO OF SQUARES

Away from the railway station towards the main square, Trg Bana Josip Jelačića are three grand public spaces. All have busy roads running down both flanks, but also boast grassy spaces, fountains and benches, making them a good place to relax and take in the scene.

Trg Kralja Tomislava **

The first square, north from the railway station, is **Trg Kralja Tomislava**, with an equestrian statue of Croatia's first king to welcome you. At the other end of Trg Kralja Tomislava is the pale yellow **Umketnički Paviljon** (Art Pavilion), constructed in 1896 as an arts space. It still hosts temporary exhibitions. Somewhat bizarrely the Pavilion was actually built in Budapest for an exhibition on the mighty Magyars and only moved south to Zagreb two years later. Look out for the sculpture by Ivan Meštrović of

Renaissance painter Andrija Medulić, which stands proudly outside near the pond and its benches. These make a good spot for admiring the sculptures and the building, also home to the eponymous Pavilion restaurant. Open Mon–Sat 11:00–19:00, Sun 10:00–13:00.

Strossmayerov trg **

Continuing north on to Strossmayerov trg you will find the **Galerija Starih Majstora** (Gallery of the Old Masters). The late Bishop Strossmayer of Đakovo's physical legacy to Zagreb was this graceful 19th-century building with its 4000 paintings, from 15th-century religious imagery through to fine works by Italian masters such as Bellini, Carpaccio and Tintoretto and on to 20th-century artists. Other features to look out for are the original 11th-century **Baška Tablet** – the oldest surviving piece of Glagolitic Script (see panel, page 89), found on the Kvarner Gulf island of Krk – and the sculpture, again by Ivan Meštrović, of Bishop Strossmayer himself. Open Wed–Sun 10:00–13:00 and 17:00–19:00, closed Mon.

Zrinjevac *

The last of the three squares is **Zrinjevac**, with its bandstand and fountain placing it firmly in the 19th century. The **Archeološki Muzej** (Archaeological Museum) is located here, with three levels of exhibits that cover various stages of the city's past, ranging from prehistoric times, through Greek dabbles on the coast and on towards the coming of the Romans. Open Tue–Fri 10:00–17:00, Sat–Sun 10:00–13:00, closed Mon.

Trg Bana Josip Jelačića **

This is the city's main square and it impresses with its numerous grand façades, pavement cafés and the rumble of both feet and trams. This is no ancient gathering place, as the city's main square once sat high above, pro-

Below: The Art Pavilion in Zagreb hosts temporary exhibitions.

Above: *The neo-Baroque National Theatre building in Zagreb.*

tected by the steep slopes of the Gornji Grad, and this space only came to the fore in 1827.

Most of the square's dramatic architecture dates from the 19th century, with some wonderfully overblown Art Nouveau façades. In the centre is a bronze equestrian statue of the eponymous Ban (the work of Antun Fernkorn), a heroic figure for Croats who see him as an early Croatian patriot who stood up to the might of the Austro-Hungarians. After World War II, when the square was renamed Trg Republike, Jelačić was secretly spirited away to a cellar and spared from certain communist destruction, with proud locals managing to hide the hefty statue away until he could make a triumphant return with Croatian independence.

Hrvatsko Narodno Kazalište (Croatian National Theatre) *

This 19th-century Austro-Hungarian creation makes a striking site in all its pastel-yellow glory. The neo-Baroque design was the work of Austrian architects Hermann Helmer and Ferdinand Fellner and outside there is a sculpture, *Well of Life*, by the ubiquitous Ivan Meštrović. The interior is more classically orientated with two grand domes adding to the ambience of this busy arts venue.

Botanical Gardens *

Zagreb's botanical gardens, dating back to the 19th century, may not win any awards, but they make a quiet oasis for those wanting to relax before catching a train from the nearby railway station. There are modest glasshouses as well as a network of small paths that meander between the flora and over ponds filled with goldfish and terrapins. In all, there are said to be over 10,000 plant species bang in the heart of the city.

JANICA KOSTELIĆ

The Zagreb-born skier, Janica Kostelić, is one of Croatia's greatest modern sporting heroes. At the age of 20 she shot to international stardom within the skiing world, when she became the first woman to win four skiing medals in one Olympics, at the 2002 Salt Lake City Winter Games. The high esteem in which Kostelić is held was illustrated when she and her father campaigned, successfully, to have Zagreb added as a venue for the Women's Skiing World Cup Alpine Slalom in 2005.

The Regent Esplanade Hotel ***

Opened in 1925, this grand old dame was one of Europe's finest hotels in the halcyon days when it caressed every need of passengers decamping from the original **Orient Express**. By the start of the new millennium it had settled into a shabby middle age, but after a major renovation it was reopened to much fanfare in 2004. Slip back through the decades by cruising past the grandiloquent neo-Classical pillars and settling in for a drink in the 1925 Cocktail Bar, or maybe just try your luck at the casino downstairs.

DONJI GRAD CULTURE
Mimara Museum **

Depending on whom you believe, this is either one of the region's finest museums, a grand gallery overflowing with top-notch art, or a cruel charade brimming with fakes. The 3750-strong personal collection of Dalmatian collector Ante 'Mimara' Topić, if you take it on face value, boasts masterpieces by the likes of Caravaggio, Degas and Manet, through to Renoir, Rembrandt and Turner, not to mention sculpture by Rodin and Robbia. Serious doubt has been cast in some quarters over the authenticity of the works in this former grammar school, but they are still (perhaps brazenly?) on display. Mimara himself died in 1987 as the gallery opened, and little is still known about his life and about how he amassed the enormous wealth to acquire such an array of paintings. Perhaps no one will ever know the reality. After all the controversy it would be criminal to miss out on seeing them for yourself. Open Tue–Sat 10:00–17:00, Thu 10:00–19:00, Sun 10:00–14:00, closed Mon.

Muzej Za Umjetnost I Obrt
(Arts and Crafts Museum) *

Another 19th-century construct, this building was the work of Herman Bollé. There are over 150,000 exhibits in an

Below: *The 19th-century Arts and Crafts Museum houses a number of themed collections.*

eclectic collage of 19 themed collections that trawl through various periods from Zagreb's past, while taking in works from other parts of Europe too. Highlights include French ivory pieces, 16th-century Italian art, and embroidery from the surrounding Gorenje region that dates back to the 15th century. The museum is also very active in organizing cultural events, educational seminars and temporary exhibitions. Open Tue–Fri 10:00–19:00, Sat–Sun 10:00–14:00, Mon closed.

Etnografski Muzej (Ethnographic Museum) *

Built in 1903, this fine Art Nouveau building only took on its current role in 1919. The museum's total stock is colossal so only a small portion of the 3000 exhibits are permanently on display. Look out for early musical instruments, lace from the Dalmatian island of Pag, Konavle jewellery, the work of Slavonian goldsmiths, traditional folk costumes (from the mainland and the islands), as well as reconstructions depicting the life of peasant people and fishermen from days gone by. Most exhibits are homegrown, but a separate section houses items from Africa, Asia and Australasia. Open Tue–Thu 10:00–17:00, Sat–Sun 10:00–13:00, closed Mon.

Below: *The funicular connecting the Donji Grad to the Gornji Grad.*

UP TO GORNJI GRAD

Getting there is all part of the fun as a quaint funicular transports those not keen on the mass of steps up from Ilica. In Gradec, the most interesting part of Gornji Grad, cobbles and crumbling old buildings abound, and there are sweeping views down over Donji Grad.

Kula Lotrščak (Lotrščak Tower) *

Be wary when you are strolling past here as there is a daily noon gun which soon sorts out the tourists from the locals, as it once did the Ottomans from the citizens of the city – it was first fired to scare off intruders. The observation level once housed troops scanning the horizon for Ottoman armies, but these days it is left to tourists soaking up panoramic views of the rooftops. One of the oldest buildings in Zagreb, it is not just a simple timepiece and viewpoint, as inside lies a modest gallery of modern art. Some of the work is for sale and there are also some gifts that make unusual souvenirs.

Strossmayerovo Šetalište (Strossmayer Parade) ★★★

This is *the* place to come for sweeping views of the Donji Grad and the cathedral. Turn right at the top of the funicular and the 19th-century terrace unfolds in a flurry of trees and benches. You can seek 'company' on the famous bench that houses the rather louche-looking figure of literary luminary Antun Gustav Matoš, the work of Croatian sculptor Ivan Kožarić.

Above: *The colourful tiled roof of St Mark's Church in Gornji Grad.*

Hrvatski Muzej Navine Umjetnosti (Gallery of Croatian Naïve Art) ★

Croatia has a strong heritage of Naïve art and here is one of the country's finest Naïve collections, said to be one of the first of its kind in Europe. Most of the artists developed organically in the countryside and it was only the efforts of collectors and exhibitors that brought their art into the city (originally the collection was known rather patronizingly as the 'Peasant Art Gallery'). Names of note to look out for amid the museum's 1500-work collection include Ivan Generalić, Franjo Mraz and Ivan Lacković. Watch out also for various temporary exhibitions. Open Tue–Fri 10:00–18:00, Sat–Sun 10:00–13:00, closed Mon.

St Mark's Church ★★★

The bright red, white and blue geometric patterns of the church's tiled roof beckon you towards this Gothic construction, but one of the country's most remarkable churches is almost as compelling inside as out. The

---

STJEPAN RADIĆ

Zagreb's Radićeva Street commemorates the life of one of Croatia's most famous politicians, Stjepan Radić (1871–1928). A staunch advocate of the Croatian state, Radić founded the Croatian Peasant Party in 1905 and led it from strength to strength, winning 67 parliamentary seats in 1925. His controversial calls for the dissolution of Croatia's union with Hungary in 1918 and his refusal to recognize the country's subsequent union with Serbia ultimately cost Radić his life – he was assassinated in Belgrade.

PETAR ZRINSKI

Former Croatian Ban, Petar Zrinksi (1621–71), is remembered fondly by Croatians. This 17th-century statesman is famous for the liberation of Croatian territory occupied by Ottoman forces and for being betrayed by the Austrian authorities. Having signed a peace treaty with Turkey, Vienna returned the land taken by Zrinksi and then publicly beheaded him, alongside Fran Krsto Frankpan (1643–71), near Vienna. Katherine's Square in Gradec is named after the ill-fated man's wife, Katrina.

tiles date from the 19th century when they were inscribed to show the emblems of Croatia, Dalmatia, Slavonia and Zagreb. Originally dating from the 13th century, St Mark's has taken on Romanesque, Gothic and Baroque touches over the centuries and withstood a litany of fires and earthquakes. Inside, the highlight is perhaps Ivan Meštrović's finest work in the capital, which depicts the Crucifixion of Christ, especially dramatic in typical stretched-out Meštrović style.

Sabor (Croatian Parliament) *

Just across from St Mark's and easily noticeable thanks to the flurry of flags, which crowd all around it, is the Croatian Parliament. This is the building in which the vital steps were taken, in June 1991, to free Croatia from Yugoslavia and become an independent nation. The Sabor paid the price of its defiance against Milosević's Yugoslavia when it was bombed by the Yugoslav air force in an attempt to assassinate President Tuđman later the same year as fighting erupted.

Atelje Meštrović (Meštrović Atelier) ***

Devotees of the legendary Croatian sculptor won't want to miss this museum, housed in the 17th-century building where he lived and based his studio between 1922 and 1942. The house and its legacy of 300 of his sculptures were one of his gifts to the capital. Exhibits include personal notes and rough sketches of some of his most seminal projects, such as the statue of *Grgur of Nin* (the original is at the northern gate of Diocletian's Palace in Split) and the *Crucifixion*, found just around the corner at St Mark's Church. The spacious gallery, styled by the sculptor himself, is stunning and you can take one of his masterpieces away with you in the form of a good-quality copy. Open Tue–Fri 10:00–18:00, Sat–Sun 10:00–14:00, closed Mon.

Below: *Sculpture of a reclining nude at the Meštrović Atelier.*

Muzej Grada Zagreba (Museum of Zagreb) **

If you want to trace the development of the city throughout the centuries then this museum, housed on this site since 1907, is the best place to start. There are a dozen main collections within the 17th-century former convent complex, with everything from 7BC artefacts recovered from archaeological digs around the city, through to various military uniforms and sculpture. Two of the most interesting recent sections deal with the war of independence in the early 1990s and how it affected the city, which was attacked on a number of occasions, and Pope John Paul II's visit to this deeply Catholic country in 1994. The scale models of the city from various periods of its history are also a useful way of getting an idea of both its development and layout. Open Tue–Fri 10:00–18:00, Sat–Sun 10:00– 13:00, closed Mon.

Above: *Zagreb Cathedral dominates the skyline of the capital.*

KAPTOL

This charming part of the city centre, easily accessible from Trg Bana Josip Jelačića, does not really lie in either the Donji or Gornji towns (lying to the north of the former and the east of the latter) and is largely given over to the machinations of the church.

Zagreb Cathedral ***

The vaulting twin towers of Zagreb's cathedral (104m and 105m high respectively) hurl themselves into many vistas of the city and you can even see them from the distant railway station on arrival. After decades of neglect an extensive renovation project began in the early 1990s and much has been done to restore the exterior to its best, although this has left it embroiled in scaffolding for years.

The gleaming gold statue of the Madonna with an entourage of angels outside is the work of architect Antun Fernkorn. Much of the rather sparse interior is neo-Gothic thanks to a major reconstruction by Herman Bollé following the earthquake of 1880 (little remains of the original 12th-century church which was ravaged by the Tartars). The main attractions for many

---

TASTE OF ZAGREB

Zagreb, like the other regions of Croatia, has its own distinctive food and drink. Locals swear by the medicinal properties of various spirits – Viljamovka (pear brandy), *travarica* (herb brandy), *šljivovica* (plum brandy) – and also recommend them interchangeably as aperitifs or digestifs. Meanwhile *Zagorski Strukli* (baked strudel with cottage cheese, browned in the oven), turkey with *mlinci* (fat-free dough made with flour and water and baked) and *orehnjaca* (walnut roll) are highly commended accompaniments to these potent tipples.

Croats are the Ten Commandments in Glagolitic Script and the tomb of controversial, but still highly revered, Zagreb Archbishop Alojzije Stepinac, which features a modest and pious sculpture by Ivan Meštrović. Look out around the cathedral for the walls that were originally designed to keep out the Ottomans.

Dolac Market **

This open market located just north up the steps from Trg Bana Josip Jelačića is a world away from staid supermarket hegemony and is known locally as the 'Belly of Zagreb'. Here, amid the colourful, bustling stalls, most of the produce is organic. Old ladies come in from the countryside to peddle their wares next to the larger resellers and you can pick up everything from flavoursome fresh fruit and vegetables right through to homemade honey. The best time to come, if you can stand the smell, is on Fridays when a bounty of fresh fish is shipped in from the Adriatic. There are a couple of informal restaurants that serve up reasonable food, with views out across the market's flurry of activity.

Kamenita Vrata (Stone Gate) *

This chunky gateway (the only one of the five city gates still standing) demarks the limits of the elevated oldest area of the Gornji Grad (known locally as Gradec) from the Kaptol. The original wooden gate, dating back to the Middle Ages, was destroyed by fire. Today's incarnation is probably from 1760, a date inscribed above the archway. A painting of the Virgin Mary is said to have survived the catastrophic fire (it can now be viewed shielded behind a grill) and hence the Stone Gate has taken on major religious and symbolic overtones, appearing in numerous Croatian stories, both aural and in written form, ever since. Look out also for the pharmacy here, said to be the second oldest in Croatia after its famous sibling down south in Dubrovnik.

1880 EARTHQUAKE

Much of Zagreb's centre owes its present-day appearance to an earthquake that rocked the city in 1880. While the quake felled many of the city's most prominent landmarks, like St Mark's Church, it also led to the revival of rundown and unsanitary areas of the city, with imposing buildings and grand boulevards replacing the previous squalor.

Below: *Lighting a candle at a shrine at Stone Gate.*

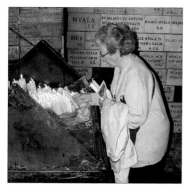

GREEN ESCAPES
Maksimir *

This sprawling park com-
plex lies a tram ride to the
east of the city centre. It
was originally planned by
Archbishop Maximilian
Maksimir (hence the
name) in the 18th century
along the lines of a traditional English-style stately
garden, and the legacy of
this are the elegant tree-lined promenades that criss-
cross its expanse, a belvedere and a sprinkling of lakes
enclosed within its boundaries. It has also evolved to
feature the unspectacular **Zagreb Zoo** and the city's
main football stadium, where both Dinamo Zagreb and
the national side play most of their matches.

Above: *The Bellevue
Pavilion in Maksimir
Park.*

Jezero Jarun (Lake Jarun) *

The centre of this green space lies at the 2km (1¼ mile)
long artificial lake that was constructed for the 1987
World Student Games. These days there are still rowing
competitions, which attract a fair crowd, but Jarun is at
its busiest in summer when the locals come to stroll
around and take in the sun. There is also a small beach
and a sprinkling of cafés. On summer nights the park
can take on a far more nefarious ambience as the city's
under-agers descend for some alcoholic revelry.

Mirogoj Cemetery **

This is a cemetery in the grand European tradition –
think Pere Lachaise in Paris or Highgate in London and
you will get the general idea. Ivan Meštrović's hand is
clearly on show again with the sculptor's dramatic
final farewell to Vladimir Becić among the lavish
cemetery's most striking tombs. Look out also for the
grave of controversial President Franjo Tuđman who
was buried here in an extravagant ceremony back in
December 1999. Other attractions include a swathe

RADIO 101

From 1983–91 the
political debates broadcast
by Zagreb's Radio 101 were
a thorn in Belgrade's side,
championing Croatian
independence and Franjo
Tuđman. Soon after he
became Croatia's first
president Tuđman himself
became one of the station's
chief critics, rejecting its
application for a new licence
in 1996. Pressure from the
Croatian public and international observers ensured that
the station was allowed to
continue its broadcasts, but
the whole incident illuminated
the fact that the country's
media was far from free.

Below: *Café culture Croatian style.*

of outdoor sculpture and the cemetery's main architect Herman Bollé's epic entrance.

Such is the grand nature of many of the graves here that some locals joke that its residents enjoy far better homes than the average living citizen. One of the best things about Mirogoj is that it is so multi-denominational with catholic Croats, orthodox Serbs, Muslims and Jews all buried in the same graveyard, and even the rugged communist-era stars allowed to remain above the graves of the once publicly venerated, but now often derided, Yugoslav-era communist apparatchiks.

Medvednica ★★★
There may no longer be any bears on 'Bear Mountain', but it is wild and green enough to make for a pleasantly bucolic escape. The rugged slopes are lined with pretty trees, but they tend to block the views from the highest peak of **Sljeme**, which reaches up to 1035m (3396ft). The mountain is a good venue for walking on the various trails and any reasonably fit adult can make it to the top, though the cable car can help less fit people on their way. In winter there is also good skiing on a number of runs and a ski school and facilities for hiring equipment. Sljeme even recently staged its first ever ski World Cup round. A good walk is 4km (2½ miles) across from Sljeme to **Medvedgrad**, a chunky fortress build to foil Tartar attacks. It never really had much foiling to do and these days it enjoys a new life as a national monument, complete with the Altar of the Homeland, where lavish state ceremonies are now conducted with sombre looking officials flocking to lay wreaths.

CAPITAL EATING AND DRINKING
With such a youthful population and a significant student demographic it comes as no surprise that

Zagreb's eating and drinking scene is vibrant to say the least. It is also very seasonal: in summer the pavement cafés abound as al fresco living becomes *de rigueur*, while in the depths of winter it is batten down the hatches time for cosy glasses of mulled wine. The worst time to come in some senses is at the height of summer when seemingly every Croat who can afford the bus fare is cooling off down on the coast, but it does mean nowhere is crowded.

Above: *Young Croatians dancing in a nightclub.*

Standards in Zagreb's restaurants are increasingly high as Croats, and visitors, start to realize their pan-national 'national cuisine' is really rather good with its Italian, Hungarian and Balkan influences and these days restaurants worthy of the name have become the norm rather than the exception.

Cafés, Bars and Restaurants

Tkalčićeva is a winding pedestrianized thoroughfare that breaks away from Trg Bana Josip Jelačića under the shadow of the Gornji Grad and is the place to see and be seen in the summer months. As soon as the sun creeps out Tkalčićeva overflows with bright young things posing their way along and on balmy spring and summer evenings during university term time it can be hard to even snare a seat despite the preponderance of venues. Bogovićeva and Preradovićev trg are another two good places to head if you are looking to enjoy some of the fine locally brewed Ozujsko beer.

If you like your meat then you will not be disappointed in the Croatian capital, with plenty of places on hand to cook you a sturdy mixed grill, some spicy sausages or maybe even a whole suckling pig! The city's restaurants have become more eclectic of late and there are now vegetarian restaurants, fine dining oases, Chinese and Indian restaurants and a range of seafood eateries, pizzerias and cafés that serve up light and healthy fare.

NIGHTLIFE

Techno, techno and more techno is the order of the day in Zagreb's club land, though the odd Latino or progressive trance night does creep in. The city's clubbing clientele are a well-dressed and critical lot so make sure to don your finest clubbing couture before hitting the dancefloor. In summer the usual clubs are often eschewed in favour of outdoor events at Lake Jarun. Current favourites of the city's clubbers include Aquarius down at Lake Jarun, Gap Club with its three dance floors, and Lapidarij.

Big international rock and pop acts often pop through Zagreb on their pan-European tours, usually playing at the Dom Sportova. The theatre and comedy scene is fairly vibrant, though often Croatian language only. One entertainment open to all: soccer games at the huge Maksimir Stadium, where local heroes Dinamo Zagreb play.

Zagreb at a Glance

May, **June** and **September** are the best months to visit when the temperature hovers above 20°C. In July and August Zagreb can become uncomfortably hot and its streets choked with traffic fumes. March, April and October are also pleasant months to visit; however, you will need some warm clothing, particularly at night. Winters can be very cold; on the upside November–February are the driest months of the year.

By Air: You can fly to Zagreb with Croatia Airlines from Dubrovnik, Split and Zadar throughout the year. There are also seasonal flights from the island of Brač. The airline's bus service will run you into the city centre for 25HRK per person, while a taxi from the airport to the city will set you back around 250HRK.
By Rail: Direct railway services link Zagreb to Karlovac, Osijek, Rijeka and Split, with plans for a new high-speed line to the latter currently being implemented. Connections are also available to and from other destinations in Croatia.
By Road: You will be able to catch a bus to any of Croatia's towns, cities and mainland tourist destinations from Zagreb. The capital is also at the heart of the country's road network.

The city centre can easily be navigated on foot; there are also a wealth of city **buses** and **trams** to choose from, as well as **taxis** and a **funicular** that links the Donji Grad (lower town) and the Gornji Grad (upper town). Tickets for use on public transport can be bought from tobacco kiosks.

LUXURY
The Regent Esplanade, Mihanovićeva 1, tel: 01 456 6666, fax: 01 456 6050, www.regenthotels.com A complete overhaul in 2004 has restored this historic monument, constructed in 1925 to accommodate the passengers on the Orient Express, to its position as Zagreb's best hotel.
Sheraton Zagreb, Kneza Borne 2, tel: 01 455 3535, fax: 01 455 3035, www.starwood.com This international chain brings large, high-tech rooms and a heated indoor swimming pool to the centre of the city.
The Westin Zagreb, Kršnjavoga 1, tel: 01 489 2000, fax: 01 489 2001, www.westin.com/zagreb High-class business oriented central hotel; comfortable rooms, eight meeting rooms.
Palace Hotel, Trg Strossmayerov 10, tel: 01 481 4611, fax: 01 481 1358, www.palace.hr The city's oldest hotel, housed inside an attractive neo-Classical building, has classically decorated and comfortable rooms. Rooms are often discounted by 20% on weekends.

MID-RANGE
Arcotel Allegra Zagreb, Branimirova 29, tel: 01 469 6000, fax: 01 469 6096, www.arcotel.cc Design hotel with light and stylish guest rooms, top-floor fitness centre and its own restaurant. Bargain rates are available through the website.
Four Points by Sheraton, Trg Sportova 9, tel: 01 363 7333, fax: 01 309 2657, www.starwood.com The comfort and services that you would expect from this international chain group have come to the former Hotel Panorama. Internet specials are often available.
Dubrovnik, Gajeva 1, tel: 01 481 8446, fax: 01 481 8447, www.hotel-dubrovnik. htnet.hr Good-sized rooms in a hard-to-beat location by the main square.
Central, Kniza Branimira 3, tel: 01 484 1122, fax: 01 484 1304, www.hotel-central.hr Handy location for the railway station, with modern rooms.

BUDGET
Omladinski Youth Hostel, Petrinjska 77, tel: 01 484 1261, fax: 01 484 1269, e-mail: zagreb@hfhs.hr Large centrally located hostel.

Zagreb at a Glance

Ravince Youth Hostel, 1 Ravince 38d, tel: 01 233 2325, fax: 01 233 2325, www.ravince-youth-hostel.hr This purpose-built hostel is 4km (2½ miles) out of town. Trams 4, 11 and 12 will get you there.
Ilica, Ilica 102, tel: 01 377 7522, fax: 01 377 7722, www.hotel-ilica.hr Small, friendly hotel a short walk west of the main square; clean and modern rooms.
Jadran, Vlaška 50, tel: 01 455 3777, fax: 01 461 2151, www.hup-zagreb.hr Rates aren't rock bottom, but this is one of the most affordable hotels in the city centre.

WHERE TO EAT

Zinfandel (see Where to Stay, the Regent Esplanade). The Esplanade's signature restaurant is arguably the most elegant and contemporary dining space in Zagreb. Superb menu features Californian and Mediterranean inspired dishes.
Gallo, Hebrangova 34, tel: 01 481 4014, fax: 01 481 4013. One of the unusual starters in this up-market cellar restaurant is pasta made with black squid ink and served with fresh truffles. There is a resident pianist.
Paviljon, Trg Kralja Tomislava 22, tel: 01 481 3066, fax: 01 484 1073. This first-rate restaurant, in the Art Pavilion, fuses Italian and Croatian cuisine, serving the likes of Fillet Mignon with truffles.

Atlanta, Tkalčićeva 65, tel: 01 481 3848. Muted shades of brown and modern art prints adorn this classy restaurant. The intimate dining space is perfect for a romantic meal.
Stara Tkalča, Tkalčićeva 70, tel: 01 481 3235, fax: 01 481 3210. Step back in time in this old-world restaurant, with its wooden interior, rustic décor, and Croatian specialities.

SHOPPING

The myriad shops between the main railway station and Ilica have been recently joined by the **Branimir shopping centre**, open until 21:00 seven days a week. You can buy virtually anything you need in the Croatian capital, from designer clothing and cheap imitations, through to electrical goods and handcrafted souvenirs. For fresh produce and a small selection of traditional gifts head to the Dolac market.

TOURS AND EXCURSIONS

Daily **walking tours** led by costumed guides leave from outside the tourist information centre (see Useful Contacts),

which also organizes tours by bus and foot. Medvednica Nature Park, with its forest, cable car, historic buildings and ski runs, is easy to reach by public transport. If you want to travel further afield, seek advice from one of the city's many travel agencies such as VWM Travel Agency.

USEFUL CONTACTS

Tourist Information Centre, Trg Bana Jelačića 11, tel: 01 481 4051, www.zagreb-touristinfo.hr
Zagreb Airport, tel: 01 626 5222, www.zagreb-airport.tel.hr/zagreb-airport
Croatia Airlines, tel: 01 616 4582, www.croatiaairlines.hr
Railway Station, Trg kralja Tomislava 12, tel: 060 333 4444, www.hznet.hr
Bus Station, Avenija M. Držića, tel: 060 313 333, www.akz.hr
Branimir Centar, Draškovićeva 51, tel: 01 469 9000.
Medvednica Nature Park, tel: 01 458 6317, www.pp-medvednica.hr
VWM Travel Agency, 3 Cvjetno naselje 20, tel: 01 606 5840, www.vmd.hr

ZAGREB	J	F	M	A	M	J	J	A	S	O	N	D
AVERAGE TEMP. °C	3	5	11	15	20	23	25	25	22	15	8	3
AVERAGE TEMP. °F	37	41	52	58	68	74	78	77	71	59	47	38
HOURS OF SUN DAILY	1.8	2.9	4.1	5.4	6.9	7.4	8.6	7.9	6.1	4.3	2.2	1.5
RAINFALL mm	52	48	56	68	83	95	79	79	79	93	86	67
RAINFALL in	2.1	1.9	2.2	2.7	3.3	3.7	3.1	3.1	3.1	3.7	3.4	2.6
DAYS OF RAINFALL	7	7	8	9	10	11	8	8	7	7	8	8

3
Inland Croatia

While the coast draws the majority of people to Croatia, visitors who have already been to the country once, or those who have a bit more time on their hands, should make the effort to explore Inland Croatia. This region's myriad attractions range from rambling castles and historic old towns, through to health spas and lively cities, not to mention the Plitvice Lakes National Park.

To the west of Zagreb are the rolling **Samobor Hills**, with **Samobor** making a very good base for setting off on the region's numerous walking trails. To the north of Zagreb is the **Zagorje**, a rugged region of tree-shrouded hills and verdant valleys that marks the border with Slovenia. Dotted around amid the folds of land are a flurry of castles, including popular **Trakošćan** with its own lake, and a sprinkling of health spas. Elsewhere in this region there is the major Paleolithic site at **Krapina**, as well as Tito's birthplace at **Kumrovec** and the only city situated north of Zagreb, **Varaždin**, with its historic fortress.

Then there is the historic city of **Karlovac** to the southwest with its old quarter and nearby war museum, one of the few in the country dedicated to the 1990s war of independence. Perhaps the most outstanding feature of Inland Croatia for most people, though, is the **Plitvice Lakes National Park**. This abundant waterworld of gurgling pools, streams and lakes is truly stunning and firmly deserves its place on UNESCO's World Heritage list.

DON'T MISS

*** Plitvice Lakes National Park: water wonderland with stunning lakes and waterfalls.
*** Stari Grad Fortress, Varaždin: this historic bulwark against the Ottomans is now an engaging museum.
** Trakošćan Castle: a fairytale reconstruction in its own grounds overlooking a lake.
** Toplice Health Spas: reward weary sightseeing limbs in healing thermal waters.
** Lonjsko Polje Nature Park: wetland paradise with birds and mammals as well as indigenous flora.

Opposite: *Trakošćan Castle overlooking its lake.*

CLIMATE

The climate of Inland Croatia is, on the whole, colder and wetter than that of Zagreb, and the tourist industry all but dies out of season. In Varaždin, though, you will still find cafés and restaurants open. Summer is the best time to visit when average temperatures are 20ºC and the days are long and sunny. Unfortunately summer is also the wettest season, so bring an umbrella.

THE SAMOBOR HILLS

Just a short drive west of Zagreb lies this hilly oasis – it is better to take the quieter local road rather than the motorway for a more relaxing drive.

Samobor **

Samobor itself is a quiet town on the Gradna river with a pleasant old core. Its two main claims to fame are: being the home of Ferdo Livadić, a composer who had a seminal influence on the region in the 19th century with his pan-Slavic ideas and, perhaps more interestingly for sweet-toothed visitors, its role as the birthplace of the **kremšnita** (although Slovenes will tell you that it hails from Lake Bled). This delicious vanilla-flavoured cream cake can be savoured in any of the cafés on **Trg Kralja Tomislava**. Samobor also boasts a Town Museum, which delves into the lives of some of its most famous residents, in particular individuals involved in the proto-Yugoslav organization the Illyrian Movement that came to the fore in the first half of the 19th century.

Inland Croatia

THE ZAGORJE
Varaždin **

Breaking north and west from Zagreb towards the Hungarian and Slovenian borders brings you into the picturesque, hilly region of Zagorje. Varaždin is the biggest settlement, a proud city with its own successful soccer team, Varteks, who have made inroads in European competitions in recent years. Varaždin has

always enjoyed an influence out-
weighing its modest size thanks to its
strategic position on the roads between
Budapest, Vienna and the Balkans. The
centre of the city is awash with impressive Baroque buildings, a legacy
of the days when Varaždin's wealthy
merchants competed with each other
by commissioning ever more elaborate
buildings. Although many have now

been touched up, a lot of work remains to be done before
the city is back to its best.

Above: *The Stari Grad
fortress complex in
Varaždin.*

Highlights around Varaždin include three impressive
religious structures: the **Cathedral of the Assumption**,
which only took on the status of cathedral in 1997, the
Church of St John the Baptist, with its sweeping 54m
(177ft) high bell tower, and the **Church of the Holy
Trinity**, with its collection of Baroque paintings and a
library containing documents thought to be some of the
oldest written in the Croatian language. **Trg Kralja
Tomislava** is home to the city's oldest building, the
chunky **Town Hall**, built back in the 16th century, whose
most striking feature is the clock tower that dominates the
square. If you are lucky, the *Purgari*, the traditional guards
of the town, will be out proudly standing sentry by the
town hall. One of the finest Baroque buildings on the
square is the **Drašković Palace**, while opposite is the
Jaccomint House, an old sweet shop laden with intricate
stuccowork – look closely and you will see it contains the
name of its former owner.

Stari Grad Fortress ★★★

The number one tourist attraction in Varaždin is undoubtedly the voluminous Stari Grad fortress, which is
bidding for inclusion on UNESCO's World Heritage list.
Much work has gone into restoring what was once a
bulwark against the Ottomans and you can now easily
spend half a day exploring this sprawling complex that
stands surrounded by its own moat (now dry). Features
to look out for are exhibits such as weapons from its

THERMAL SPAS

One of Inland Croatia's best-kept secrets is its thermal spas, whose mineral-rich thermal waters and mud compounds are believed to have healing properties. Relaxation programmes, comprising bathing, whirlpools, saunas and massage, are offered alongside medical treatments aimed at helping those who suffer from ailments such as rheumatism and spinal complaints, as well as neurological, respiratory and heart problems. The Croatian National Tourist Board (www.croatia.hr) has a comprehensive list of health resorts on its website.

militarized past as well as old bullet-marked hunting targets dating from the 19th century. **St Lovro Chapel** meanwhile has to be one of the few chapels in the world built with wide slits for enabling canons to fire out of it. In the bowels of the fortress is an exhibition space, often used for displaying the work of local artists. Open Tue–Fri 10:00–15:00, Sat–Sun 10:00–13:00.

Zagorje Castles

Hiring a car is definitely the best way to explore the winding roads of the Zagorje as the local bus and train services are not convenient for sightseeing.

Trakošćan Castle **

East of Varaždin towards the Slovenian border is Trakošćan Castle, a bright white fortification set amidst trees and overlooking its own lake. The original dates from the 12th century, but today's much visited creation is largely the work of the Draškovic dynasty who took the reins in the 16th century and proceeded to spend four centuries remoulding it, with much of the most visible work dating from the 19th century. Today the castle also houses a museum that looks into the various stages of its past and that of the seminal Draškovic family. The man-made lake below has a path that allows a lazy meander around, with pedalos on hand for anyone wanting to get closer to the water. Look out for wild deer who often wander around the lake.

Below: *The arched corridor at Trakošćan Castle north of Zagreb.*

Veliki Tabor *

An equally attractive fortification lies to the west: the Veliki Tabor. Formerly a stronghold of the Counts of Celje, the once mighty dynasty from neighbouring Slovenia, the sturdy looking castle overlooks the surrounding countryside from a grassy hill. The signature orange-roofed semicircular towers date from the 16th century, and the extensive collection of weapons and costumes displayed in the castle's various exhibition rooms, spread across the centuries, mark various periods in the castle's eclectic history. Some of the most interesting exhibits are the items focusing on the World War II Partisan resistance in the Zagorje.

AROUND THE ZAGORJE
Krapina *
South of Trakošćan and Veliki Tabor is the sleepy town of Krapina, which rose to international fame thanks to the discovery of

Above: *The dramatic Veliki Tabor castle.*

Krapina Man in the late 19th century. Atop a hilly rise are the remains of a Palaeolithic site that revealed skeletons and artefacts dating back to around 40,000 years ago, when early man is thought to have inhabited the surrounding caves. Many of the oldest bones were spirited off to Zagreb long ago, but there is still the **Museum of Evolution** which is worth a visit, as is the hill itself with its sculptures revealing what life would have been like back then, complete with depictions of Neanderthal man and vicious looking bears.

Kumrovec **
Another famous man is remembered in nearby Kumrovec, this time the leader who ruled Yugoslavia for four decades, **Josef Broz 'Tito'**. The Croat was born into a local peasant family here in 1892 and many of his first socialist meetings were held away from prying eyes in the surrounding hills. A modest museum and striking statue mark the site of his old house with little more than a sprinkling of family possessions on display, and if you are coming here anyway it is worth popping into the surrounding memorial to Tito in the form of the original village houses that have been restored to depict peasant life in the 19th and early 20th centuries.

KRAPINA MAN

Between 1899 and 1905, over 870 fossilized remains of Neanderthal Man were unearthed at Hušnjak Hill, a dig that elevated this sleepy area to one of the foremost Neanderthal sites in the world. Under the guidance of Croatian geologist, Dragutin Gorjanović-Kramberger, the team excavated lower jaw-bones complete with sets of teeth, and fragments of human skeletons. Experts believe that this might have been the burial site of around 80 people.

Above: *The grey heron, one of the many bird species found at Lonjsko Polje Nature Park.*

Health Spas **

A more relaxing option is visiting the newly revamped **Krapinske Toplice** health spa, which was built in the late 19th century. Spread across this lotus-eating complex are a dozen hot pools, ranging from pleasantly lukewarm, where you can swim if you like, through to what seems like boiling point, as well as mud baths. While most casual visitors come to relax, there is a serious side to it all as many locals come here for specific health issues, such as stress, skin diseases and cardiac problems. The thermal waters are laced with calcium and magnesium, which give them their healing properties. Other spas in the Zagorje include **Sutinske Toplice**, **Tuheljske Toplice**, **Stubiće Toplice** and one in Varaždin itself. All of the Zagorje's spas are within easy driving distance of the capital, making them perfect for stressed-out city dwellers and tourists alike.

EAST OF ZAGREB
Lonjsko Polje Nature Park **

Lying to the east of Zagreb, between the towns of Nova Gradiška and Sisak, are the **Lonjsko Polje wetlands** on the banks of the mighty Sava River. Long a favourite of local ornithologists, one of Europe's largest wetland oases rose to more widespread attention when it was designated a nature reserve in 1990, though the almost immediate onset of the war retarded its growth. Among the many **bird species** that can be seen are **spoonbills**, **herons**, **harriers**, **egrets**, **white-tailed eagles** and, the most famous resident, **black storks**, who cruise in from Africa in spring and usually hang around until the first chill winds of October. Other fauna includes **wild deer**, **boar**, **Turopolje pigs** and **Posavina horses**. Even if you are not interested in the wealth of flora and fauna, the quaint wooden villages of **Lonjsko Polje** are worth meandering around on a day trip from Zagreb, or as a scenic detour en route to Eastern Croatia.

LONJSKO POLJE WALKING TRAILS

Those wanting to learn more about Lonjsko Polje Nature Park are invited to follow one or both of two self-guided walking trails. **The Secrets of the Čigoč Triangle** and **The Posavac Trail** take around 90 minutes each. Leaflets detailing the routes can be picked up from Čigoč 26 in the village of the same name.

Jasenovac *

This former concentration camp, a short drive east of Lonjsko Polje, remains one of the most disturbing places in Croatia. The fact that it is so low key and that the small visitor centre is closed at weekends reveals much about the embarrassment and shame it causes amongst many Croats and also, more worryingly, about the degree of denial that still surrounds Croatian atrocities committed during World War II.

Jasenovac is little more than a massive grass void, whose sheer size gives some idea of the scale of murderous regime here. During World War II the local Ustaše fascists were only too keen to follow the example of their German masters, and Jews, Serbs, political prisoners and other 'undesirables' were brought here ostensibly for imprisonment, though many died from disease or were killed. The exact number of deaths remains the subject of some controversy, with numbers ranging from 70,000 through to one million. A section of the site is dominated by a huge rose-shaped memorial designed by the artist Bogdan Bogdanović.

> **USTAŠE**
>
> Established in 1929, the Ustaše were essentially a far-right political organization that espoused the virtues of extreme Croatian nationalism and employed terrorist tactics. In 1941, during World War II, the Germans placed the Ustaše at the helm of the puppet Croatian state. Pursuing the goals of Nazism, the Ustaše, led by Ante Pavelić, established the Jasenovac concentration complex – a collection of eight camps – and orchestrated the killing of thousands of political prisoners, Serbs and Jews.

SOUTH OF ZAGREB
Karlovac **

During the 1990s the largely industrial city of Karlovac, a short hop southwest down the motorway from Zagreb, marked the front line. Subsequently the city was repeatedly attacked by Serb forces who lobbed shells in with little regard as to whether they hit civilian or military targets. War damage is slowly being repaired and the local tourist authorities are very keen to attract visitors again.

The main attraction in Karlovac is the Austro-Hungarian era **Old Town**, with its crumble of buildings a legacy of the days when the city was a crucial part of the massive Krajina military stronghold, which was designed

Below: *Karlovac's Old Town centre.*

to keep the Ottoman hordes at bay by preventing them from crossing the Kupa and Korana rivers and marching onwards towards the gates of Vienna. Karlovac did not even exist until the 16th century when it came into being purely as a military creation in a six-star design. The award-winning **Town Museum** delves into the city's and the Krajina's history with a collage of military uniforms, weapons and even a model of the original star-shaped fortress. Walking around the old quarter you can also see the drained moats and imagine what it must have looked like when the mighty bastion was an essential part of the Krajina. Open Tue–Fri 08:00–15:00, Sat–Sun 10:00–12:00.

Turanj **

On the southern outskirts of Karlovac is Turanj, which has one of the country's few museums dedicated to the 1990s war of independence. The **open-air museum** features a motley collection of vehicles and cannons, revealing just how patched together and heroic the local attempt to hold off one of Europe's most powerful armies was. Amongst the exhibits are a converted tractor with hastily attached armoured plating and an old Russian howitzer, not what you would imagine to be ideal for tackling Yugoslav tanks. Many of the Croatian forces were policemen rather than trained soldiers as well as completely untrained volunteers, but they somehow managed to hold the front line here, not without paying a bitter cost, though, as the memorial that lies across the road from the museum testifies.

Below: *This memorial in Turanj has a list of the local war dead.*

Plitvice Lakes National Park ***

Lying between Karlovac and the coast is the Plitvice Lakes National Park, one of Europe's great green spaces and Croatia's most popular tourist attraction:

in short, an essential stop. Placed on **UNESCO's World Heritage** list back in 1979, the lakes are justifiably popular with domestic and international visitors. In all, 16 lakes fan out across this natural tree-shrouded playground, with a network of paths, bridges, raised walkways, stairs, boats and tourist trains all on hand to ferry people around as efficiently as possible while limiting the damaging effect of so many visitors.

Thankfully today there is little sign of the destruction done by Serb forces who senselessly ransacked and vandalized the park during the Croatian war of independence. There is a trio of hotels inside the park's boundaries and staying the night is a good idea to avoid having to fight for a space in the public car parks. An overnight stay also allows you to appreciate the park once the crowds have dispersed; this is especially appealing at the height of summer when the park reaches saturation point during the day. Out of season the park takes on a very different hue and it is simply stunning in winter.

There is one admission fee, which grants you access to the entire park and also includes the boats and tourist trains. There are numerous highlights as you skirt one emerald lake after another and the spray from the waterfalls mists your face, but it can all get a bit too much in high season with fellow visitors jockeying for the best photo opportunities and, much worse, breaking bits off the fragile rock face and leaving the marked paths for a bit of impromptu exploring. If it gets too much, head to the park's extremity and **Lake Proščansko**, a green lung with relatively few visitors. This is the park's largest stretch of water and it is a wonderfully relaxing place to be on a warm summer's day, giving you time to kick back and appreciate the scenery.

Above: *Plitvice Lakes National Park, an oasis of waterfalls and lakes.*

WAR IN PLITVICE LAKES NATIONAL PARK

Forty-two years after becoming Croatia's first national park, the Plitvice Lakes experienced the darkest days of their history. On Easter Sunday 1991 the first shots of the Homeland War were fired in the park. The first human fatality also occurred here, when park official and Croat Josip Jovic was shot. Serbs occupied the park until 1995, but today it is back to its peaceful best, welcoming hundreds of thousands of visitors each year.

Back on the main route, the 8km (5 miles) of lakes are split between the upper and lowers lakes. The aforementioned Lake Proščansko is at the upper extremity to the south and the Labudovac Falls connect it with the rest of the network of lakes. Heading north you come to **Lake Galovac** and then down into **Lake Gradinsko** from where it is a short walk to **Lake Kozjak**, the main lake as it were, with boats on hand to ferry visitors back towards the main entrance with its hotels and restaurants, and also across to the rest of the lower lakes. The highlight of the lower lakes is **Veliki Slap** (or 'big waterfall'), which gushes impressively and makes for great photos.

The Plitvice Lakes' **flora and fauna**, as you might expect, are both varied and bountiful. In recent years wild bears have become a problem, as they seem to enjoy traipsing around wherever they fancy on the scrounge for food (including petrol station forecourts), which can be a terrifying but memorable experience for tourists.

Also present here are over 150 bird species, including **eagles**, **peregrine falcons** and **tawny owls**, as well as **wild boar**, **lynx**, **otters**, **wild cats** and even **wolves**.

Below: *Walkways lead visitors through Plitvice National Park.*

Inland Croatia at a Glance

April–September are the best months to visit, when the temperature hovers around 20°C (68°F). Winter is very cold. The economy of Inland Croatia is much less dependent on tourism than along the coast, with hotels and restaurants open year-round.

By Rail: There is a direct rail link connecting Zagreb, Karlovac and Varaždin.
By Road: The most practical way to travel around Central Croatia is by car. Buses run between Zagreb and all the destinations in Inland Croatia, though they are not as well connected to each other. From Varaždin you can catch a bus to Trakošćan.

All the destinations in this chapter can be explored on foot, except the Samobor Hills, where you will need a car. Karlovac and Varaždin both have bus services, but tourists seldom use them. Visitors to Plitvice Lakes National Park use boats and tourist trains as well as walking trails.

Samobor
Livadić, Trg Kralija Tomislava 5, tel: 01 336 5850, fax: 01 336 5851, www.hotel-livadic.hr Plush by the standards of other accommodations in Inland Croatia.

Trakošćan
Trakošćan Hotel, tel: 042 796 224, www.hotel.hr/coning Large business hotel located close to Trakošćan castle.
Varaždin
Hotel Turist, Aleja Kralija Zvonimira 1, tel: 042 395 395, fax: 042 214 479, www.hotel-turist.hr Business hotel, good facilities, central.
Krapinske Toplice
Toplice Hotel, tel: 049 232 165, fax: 049 232 322. The spa's own hotel is a large concrete offering, but well located.
Karlovac
Carlstadt, Vraniczanyeva 2, tel: 047 611 111, www.carlstadt.hr The city's only real hotel; has decent rooms.
Plitvice Lakes
Hotel Jezero, tel: 053 751 400, www.np-plitvicka-jereza.hr Enjoy the park with a lake-view room in Plitvice's most luxurious hotel.

Trakošćan
Trakošćan Hotel (*see* Where to Stay). Passable tourist fare.
Varaždin
Tempio, Prešernova 3, tel: 042 210 136. Italian and Istrian

influences abound. Opt for anything served with truffles.
Plitvice Lakes
Hotel Jezero (*see* Where to Stay). Outdoor terrace and decent Croatian staples.
Samobor
Samoborska Pivnica, Šmidhenova 3, tel: 01 336-1623. Beer hall serving cheap and hearty meat dishes.

Krapina Tourist Information, Magistratska 11, tel: 049 371 330.
Karlovac Tourist Information, Petra Zrinskog 3, tel: 047 615 115, fax: 047 600 602, www.karlovac-touristinfo.hr
Krapinske Toplice Tourist Information, Zagrebacka 2, tel: 049 232 106.
Samobor Tourist Information, Trg kralija Tomislava 5, tel: 01 336 0044, www.samobor.hr
Varaždin Tourist Information, Ivana Padovca 3, tel: 042 210 987, fax: 042 210 985, www.tourism-varazdin.com
Plitvice Lakes National Park, tel: 053 751 015, fax: 053 751 013, www.np-plitvice.hr
Trakošćan Castle, tel: 042 796 422, www.trakoscan.net

VARAŽDIN	J	F	M	A	M	J	J	A	S	O	N	D
AVERAGE TEMP. °C	1	1	6	10	16	18	20	20	16	10	4	1
AVERAGE TEMP. °F	32	35	44	51	61	66	69	68	62	51	40	35
HOURS OF SUN DAILY	1.7	2.7	3.8	4.7	5.2	6.0	7.6	7.2	5.5	4.1	1.9	1.4
RAINFALL mm	40	40	40	70	90	90	100	90	70	70	80	50
RAINFALL in	1.8	1.7	1.9	2.9	3.6	3.8	4.3	3.8	2.9	2.8	3.4	2.3
DAYS OF RAINFALL	6	6	6	9	11	12	12	11	7	6	6	6

4
Eastern Croatia

Eastern Croatia, much of it a fertile plain stretching across Slavonia towards the Serbian border, was the worst affected region during the 1990s war of independence. In particular the town of **Vukovar** became the focus of Croatia's desperate struggle against Serb forces and the supposedly neutral Yugoslav National Army. Many social and economic problems remain, with the Croats and their Serb neighbours still bitterly divided; this is unsurprising when you consider that many Serbs fled to Serbia or fought for the Serbian side. The region is, however, safe for tourists.

One of the highlights of culturally rich Eastern Croatia is the elegant city of **Osijek**, whose cosmopolitan buzz is slowly returning and which also boasts the historic quarter of **Trvđa**. **Slavonski Brod**, with its fortress complex, is also worth visiting. Vukovar, which remains the most scarred by the war of independence, is an essential stop for those with more than a passing interest in the conflict. Away from the towns and cities are the vineyards of **Ilok**, now recovering after being senselessly vandalized by Serb forces, and the bucolic splendour of **Kopački Rit**, an oasis of flora and fauna, now back to its best.

The **people** are often what makes a visit to Eastern Croatia so special. The Croats genuinely welcome anyone coming back to a region in such desperate need of investment and embrace those showing an interest in a conflict that during the dark days of 1991–92 left them feeling as if the rest of Europe had abandoned them.

DON'T MISS

*** Trvđa, Osijek: Osijek's atmospheric quarter comes complete with stunning Baroque architecture and lively bars.
** Cathedral of St Peter, Đakovo: Imposing red brick Gothic cathedral with stunning frescoes.
** Kopački Rit Nature Park: this wetland retreat is an ornithologist's dream.

Opposite: *War Memorial to the Siege of Vukovar in the early 1990s.*

CLIMATE

Eastern Croatia's economy isn't dependent on tourism so restaurants, cafés, bars and hotels open year-round. In winter the climate can be harsh, with highs averaging 1ºC and feeling even colder in the wind or rain. A veil of snow also covers the ground for much of the season. Late spring through to early autumn is a good time to visit, with pleasant temperatures and no fear of being overrun by tourists.

HEADING EAST
Slavonski Brod *

Heading east from Zagreb along the pancake flat motorway (known locally as the *autocesta*) the attractions of Eastern Slavonia can seem a long way away, so a good stop is at the town of Slavonski Brod on the banks of the River Sava. The quisling state of Serbian Bosnia lies just across the river and during the war of independence Slavonski Brod paid a heavy price with shelling and sniping from the other side of the Sava.

Today Slavonski Brod is back on its feet though there is little to actually see and do. There is a sprinkling of decent cafés, bars and restaurants for a refreshment stop and one major site – the sprawling 18th-century **Brod Fortress**, which is the legacy of the days when the town stood as a bulwark against the Ottomans. Some money has recently been invested in the site to make it part of the town's museum, although much work still needs to be done. It is also possible to walk along the northern banks of the Sava to the old **Franciscan Monastery**, which dates from the 18th century and has recently been revamped.

Below: Đakovo Cathedral, the legacy of Bishop Strossmayer.

Đakovo **

You know you are getting close to Đakovo when the vaulting twin spires of its landmark cathedral lurch into view across the Slavonian plain. Once a Turkish enclave – the small mosque is the only lasting reminder – Đakovo was the home town of influential Croatian Bishop Strossmayer and his legacy is this dramatic cathedral. The **Cathedral of St Peter**, the work of Viennese architects, was built in the second half of the 19th century. The two huge 84m (276 ft) high bell towers are its most striking features. The interior also includes frescoes attributed to Ljudevit Seitz and sculptures by Tomas Vodcka, while the crypt is the last resting place of the famous bishop himself.

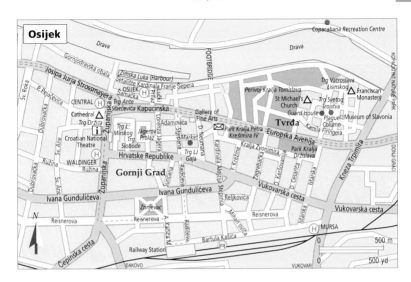

OSIJEK

The largest settlement in Eastern Croatia, Osijek has a stately Central European feel, with rumbling trams and buildings that boast grand façades and impressive Art Nouveau architecture. It was badly damaged during the war of independence and, after the fall of Vukovar, was in serious danger of falling to Serb forces. Thankfully the city held out and most of its Baroque centre and the impressive Trvđa quarter survived. Tragically around 1000 of Osijek's inhabitants lost their lives during the conflict.

City Centre **

Osijek is split neatly into the Gornji (upper) and Donji (lower) towns, as well as Trvđa. Most of the city centre is comprised of **Gornji Grad** (the Upper Town), home to an array of interesting buildings. The most striking height-wise is the vaulting neo-Gothic **cathedral**, commissioned, like the cathedral in Đakovo, by Slavonian Bishop Strossmayer and largely built using red bricks. Nearby the **Croatian National Theatre** is a stunningly ornate building. Bombed by the Serbs, the theatre has only recently been returned to its best with the perhaps

> ### LANDMINES
>
> The Yugoslav National Army (JNA) and irregular Serbian forces occupied large swathes of Croatia between 1991 and 1998. One hazardous consequence of the war was the mining of the front lines. Although the Croatian government has worked hard to remove land-mines, especially in tourist areas, some do remain. These are at their most obvious in Slavonia, where signs sporting skulls and bones alongside the word 'mine', warn of the danger, but can also be found in mountainous areas through-out the country – so be careful and don't stray off marked paths.

Above: *The heart of Trvda and Osijek – Trg Svetog Trojstva.*

unlikely help of international fast food chain McDonalds. The price of this assistance, of course, was letting them open up a branch on the site.

Europska *

Much of Osijek's finest archi-tecture is found on the elegant thoroughfare of Europska. The impressive row of Art Nouveau façades has largely been re-paired since the war. During Osijek's cosmopolitan heyday wealthy Austrians, Germans and Hungarians lavished money on ever more elaborate homes in an attempt to outdo one another. Continuing along Europska, heading away from the city, allows you to delve into two of Osijek's parks (the city has no fewer than 17), before you reach the historic quarter of Trvda.

Trvda ***

The Austro-Hungarians conjured up the Trvda complex back in the 18th century as one of their greatest barriers against the Ottomans. Its many **Baroque buildings** used to house soldiers' barracks, officers' quarters and the storerooms, military academies and churches that went with them. Until the war of independence the Yugoslav National Army resided here; their thanks during the fight-ing was to shell the complex from the opposite bank of the Drava River. The authorities in Osijek are currently in the midst of an attempt to get Trvda placed on UNESCO's World Heritage list, a move that would bring much needed funds for restoration, a task which, at the moment, is largely being undertaken by the Catholic Church. So far the church has helped reconstruct **St Michael's Church** and the **Franciscan Monastery**.

Trvda is easy to explore. The main focal point is **Trg Svetog Trojstva**, an expansive cobbled square lined with elegant buildings such as the **Guard House** with its

---

SLAVONIAN CUISINE

Menus in the Eastern Croatian region of Slavonia are influenced by its geo-graphical location, with warming Hungarian stews and hearty Balkan meat dishes being staple foods, especially during the region's long and cold winters. Slavonian specialities include *kulen* (a spicy salami prepared using traditional methods and frequently served with fresh vegetables and creamy cheese) and *Fiš paprikaš*, a spicy fish stew made with freshwater fish such as carp.

clock tower, colonnades and cannons, the **Museum of Slavonia**, featuring Roman artefacts and various other exhibits from the city's eclectic past, and the **University Rectorate**. In the centre of the square is a **plague column** said to have been commissioned by the wife of a local commander in thanks for the city being spared from the worst ravages of an outbreak of the dreaded disease. These days the students returning to the increasingly busy bars of this atmospheric historic quarter also seem to be thankful of their elegant old world surroundings.

The Banks of the River Drava *

In the city centre the banks of the Drava around the landmark Hotel Osijek are once again filling with students and a smattering of tourists, who defy the mosquitoes and recline among the outdoor cafés and floating restaurants. Walkways and cycle paths break away from the centre and on a roasting summer's day you can even bathe in the river water. The best place for a dip is Osijek's very own **Copacabana**, a leisure complex with pools, 'beaches' and snack bars. It may not be as glamorous as its Brazilian namesake, but on a hot day it is a fun place to be.

VUKOVAR

For a few months in 1991 Vukovar was Croatia's Stalingrad. The population of this once graceful Baroque town cowered in their basements without electricity, or fresh food and water, as a piecemeal but heroic defence of local volunteers, police and hastily assembled National Guard forces managed to stand up to the tanks, fighter bombers and howitzers of the Yugoslav

OVČARA AND THE HAGUE

In October 1995 three Serb generals – Mile Mrkšić, Miroslav Radić and Veselin Šljivančanin – were indicted by The Hague for war crimes in relation to the mass grave uncovered at Ovčara. The generals stand accused of the execution of 260 Croats, in what has come to be regarded as one of the biggest atrocities of the Homeland War. Five other people have also been indicted in relation to the Ovčara murders.

National Army and Serbian paramilitary volunteers. The defence of Vukovar was played out nightly on Croatian TV, but the European Community failed to act. On 18 November the inevitable happened and the town fell. Serb forces and the dreaded Četnik paramilitaries funnelled into the shell of a town. What happened next was one of the most savage acts of the 1990s Balkan wars as hundreds of patients were snatched by Serb forces from under the noses of the International Red Cross and spirited off to a field in nearby Ovčara where they were murdered in cold blood. All in all over 1000 people are still missing from around the Vukovar area.

Over a decade on, finally Serbian soldiers and paramilitaries are now facing war crimes charges in The Hague, but the damage, both physical and psychological, still hangs over Vukovar like a troubled ghost. The once Croat majority town now has more Serbs than Croats, Serb and Croat children go to separate classes at the same school and the population has so far reached only around a third of pre-war levels.

Legacy of the War **

In view of such a grim past the question may be asked, 'Why go to Vukovar?' The answer quite simply is that the local Croat people want you to recognize what happened there, help to ensure that it will never happen again, and also aid the town's economic recovery. The effects of the war, slowly being patched up with a trickle of international aid, are still all too evident even on the walls of the town's only hotel and in the main streets where some buildings are mere shells of their former selves. The damaged water tower, a symbol of the siege of Vukovar for many Croats, is to be left in its scarred state as a permanent memorial. Two other moving memorials are the dignified **war cemetery**

Below: *War Cemetery marking the Serb massacre of Croats at Ovčara.*

on the outskirts of the town that houses both combatants and civilians, and the stark monument at **Ovčara** a few miles further on, which marks where Serbian forces butchered and buried the Croats snatched from Vukovar's hospital at the end of the siege.

Eltz Palace ★★

The only two real tourist sights as such are the **Monastery** and **Eltz Palace**. The latter, a once graceful Baroque manor lying in lush grounds overlooking the Danube, was hammered by Serbian shelling and many of its artistic and cultural treasures were hauled off as booty to Serbia in the 1990s. The recovery has been slow but thanks to some international funding, to help both with the renovation of the building and the acquisition of new exhibits, as well as an agreement with the Serbs to start returning some of the stolen property, the palace is slowly dragging itself back from near annihilation. Today it hosts the **Town Museum** with old folk costumes and paintings among the exhibits, as well as occasional showcases of local art.

Above: *War damage to buildings in the centre of Vukovar.*

Franciscan Monastery ★

The town's most dramatic religious building, which overlooks Vukovar from its own bluff above the Danube and dates back to the 18th century, was virtually flattened by the Serbs, but it has been impressively rebuilt since 1998. While the exterior may have taken on a bright new sheen it is still pretty bare on the inside.

AROUND EASTERN SLAVONIA
Ilok ★

Before the war Croatia's most easterly town on the banks of the mighty River Danube was renowned for the quality of its **white wine**, produced in its bountiful vineyards, which had been flowing since Roman times. All that changed during the war of independence

> **ROCKY RIDE FOR THE CROATIAN LANGUAGE**
>
> Throughout history the Croatian language has fallen in and out of favour. In the 10th century Pope Ivan IX forbade clergymen to celebrate mass in Croatian. It also played second fiddle to Serbian in the Serbo-Croat lexicon that was used in Yugoslavia. However, Ante Pavelić decreed in 1941 that people could only speak the purest form of Croatian, and since 1991 efforts have been made to purge Serbian words from the language.

when Serb forces 'ethnically cleansed' local Croats and set about destroying the vineyards. No wine was produced until after the region had been handed back to Croatia in 1998.

Ilok enjoys an enviable position overlooking the Danube. The remains of an old fortress are worth visiting even if it is only because you have developed an understandable love of the fine dry white wine. Within the sturdy old walls is the 15th-century **Church of St Ivan**, which has recently undergone renovation. Look out also for the nearby remains of the old **Arab Baths**, a legacy of the days when the Ottomans held sway over Ilok. Also worth popping into is the **Town Museum**, housed in an impressive pastel pink 17th-century mansion, the **Odescalchi Manor**.

Kopački Rit Nature Park **

The weight of recent history can become a little overwhelming in Eastern Croatia and if it does you can always visit the Kopački Rit Nature Park just a short drive north of Osijek. This protected wetland area of 181km^2 (70 sq miles) was set up in the 1960s and survived being stomped over and mined by Serbian forces during the war. It is the last watery flourish of the Drava River before it is swallowed up by the mighty Danube. It is constantly evolving, often drying to a trickle, before heavy rains sweep in and it explodes with flora and fauna as colour and life return to a parched landscape.

Highlights of the park include the **black storks**, **grey herons**, **white-tailed eagles**, **cormorants** and **crested grebes**, as well as **deer** and **wild boar**. In the waters of the park lurk around 50 fish species. The best time to visit is normally between spring and autumn when the Drava's water is high.

Below: *An egret glides serenely, reflected in the tranquil water.*

Eastern Croatia at a Glance

BEST TIMES TO VISIT

Eastern Croatia has a continental climate with warm **summers** (Jun–Aug) and mild temperatures in **May** and **Sep**. From Nov–Mar the temperature plummets, rarely rising above freezing. Snow covers the ground for much of winter.

GETTING THERE

By Air: During the summer Croatia Airlines operates domestic flights to Osijek from Split and Dubrovnik.
By Rail: A direct rail service connects Osijek to Zagreb and Rijeka.
By Road: An underused motorway runs between Zagreb and Đakovo. Buses take you to Osijek, Vukovar and Đakovo from Zagreb. There are also shorter distance bus services between towns and cities in Eastern Croatia. To visit the nature parks you will need a car.

GETTING AROUND

Vukovar, Đakovo and Osijek have city bus services, with the latter also having a tram network. These are seldom used by tourists.

WHERE TO STAY

Osijek
Hotel Osijek, Šamačka 4, tel: 031 201 333, fax: 031 212 135. A much-needed revamp has removed the bullet holes and pockmarks; today the hotel is pleasant with many rooms offering river views.

Vukovar
Hotel Dunav, Trg Republike Hrvatske 1, tel: 032 441 285, fax: 032 441 762. The town's only hotel has functional rooms. Book a Danube view.

Đakovo
Croatia Turist, Preradovićeva 25, Đakovo, tel: 031 813 391, fax: 031 814 319. Central hotel with good rooms.

Slavonski Brod
Hotel Park, Trg Pobjede 1, tel: 031 410 228, fax: 031 442 306. Small, central hotel with its own restaurant.
Hotel – Vinarija Zdjelarevic, Vinogradska 102, Brod Stupnik, tel; 035 427 775, fax: 035 427 040, www.zdjelarevic.hr If you have your own wheels, head to the Brod countryside for real Slavonian hospitality, complete with modern rooms, great views and a wine cellar.

WHERE TO EAT

Osijek
El Paso, tel: 031 203 500. Popular pizzeria, permanently moored on the Drava. It is also one of the most popular nightspots in the city.
Slavonska Kuća, Kamila Firingera 26, tel: 031 208

277. Atmospheric Trvta eatery serving spicy Hungarian-influenced dishes.
Vukovar
Hotel Dunav (*see* Where to Stay). Dining options in this war-scarred town are scarce, but the hotel's restaurant or café are a good bet.
Đakovo
Croatia Turist (*see* Where to Stay). Hearty Slavonian specialities washed down with local wines in the shadow of the town's fine cathedral.

USEFUL CONTACTS

Osijek Tourist Information, Županijska 2, tel: 031 203 755, fax: 031 203 749, www.tzosijek.hr
Vukovar Tourist Information, J. J. Stossmayera 15, tel: 032 442 889, fax: 032 442 889.
Đakovo Tourist Information, Kralija Tomislava 3, tel: 031 812 319.
Kopački Rit Nature Park, Petefi 35, Bilje, tel: 031 750 855, fax: 031 750 755, www.kopacki-rit.com
Lonjske Polje Nature Park, Trg Kralija P, Svacica, tel: 044 672 080, www.pp-lonjsko-polje.hr

OSIJEK	J	F	M	A	M	J	J	A	S	O	N	D
AVERAGE TEMP. °C	1	1	7	11	16	19	21	20	17	11	5	1
AVERAGE TEMP. °F	32	35	45	52	62	67	71	69	63	53	41	35
HOURS OF SUN DAILY	1.8	2.8	4.1	5.0	5.5	6.2	7.7	7.3	5.6	4.3	1.6	1.5
RAINFALL mm	45.5	41.8	45.3	59.8	69.2	81.8	60.8	57.6	54.3	60.1	61.3	54.7
RAINFALL in	1.79	1.65	1.78	2.35	2.72	3.22	2.4	2.23	2.1	2.37	2.41	2.15
DAYS OF RAINFALL	12.2	11.1	11.5	12.6	13.2	12.6	10.2	9.4	8.9	10.4	12.7	14

5
Istria

Istria, the peninsula that juts out into the northern Adriatic, was popular with holiday-makers from countries like Austria, Germany and the United Kingdom as early as the 1960s. Tito earmarked Istria for mass tourism and it is easy to see why, since it has an idyllic climate, clean seas and a sprinkling of coastal towns. The war barely touched Istria and today it is once again popular not only with the package tour crowds, but also with independent travellers wanting to explore the little-heralded interior.

Istria has shifted back and forth between Croatian and Italian control and the legacy of the region is an Italian-speaking population, dual-language road signs and inhabitants with an incurable addiction to first-rate pizza and ice cream. In the historic centres of **Pula**, **Rovinj** and **Poreč** the Latin strain re-emerges with Roman remnants including Pula's stunning amphitheatre and Poreč's remarkable Basilica of St Euphrasius. Poreč is also a package tour favourite, a smooth functioning resort that can cater for as many as 700,000 tourists a year.

Away from the Adriatic coast and its resorts, **inland Istria** has recently been lauded in the travel press as the 'New Tuscany' and it does indeed have many similarities to the Italian region, with its rolling vine-strewn hills, excellent wine, high-quality truffles and the sort of gorgeous hill towns complete with orange roof tiles that tend to get both tourists and property speculators very excited.

DON'T MISS

*** Roman Amphitheatre, Pula: one of the largest in the world and atmospheric for live performances.
*** Basilica of Euphrasius, Poreč: don't miss this magnificent Byzantine basilica.
*** Grožnjan: attractive hill-top town in inland Istria, given a new lease of life by artists and musicians.
** Motovun: Gothic, Venetian, Renaissance and Romanesque architecture.
*** Rovinj: an Italianate gem atop a rocky outcrop.
*** Beram: see the dramatic *Danse Macabre* frescoes in the Church of St Mary.

Opposite: *The Roman Arch in central Pula.*

PULA

Dismiss Pula, Istria's only city, as a grimy port and ramshackle place at your peril, as below the raffish exterior lurks an intriguing Roman legacy with that iconic landmark **Roman Amphitheatre** only the start. The city also boasts a sprinkling of bars, cafés and restaurants, and the green oasis of the **Veruski Kanal Inlet** lies just around the bay to the south.

Roman Amphitheatre ★★★

The days when gladiators clashed their swords or baited lions may be long gone, but on a balmy summer's night when 23,000 spectators crowd in, it is easy to feel the depth of history in this 1st century AD amphitheatre knowing that the seat you are on was once warmed by a Roman rear. Pula's Roman arena, one of the largest left standing in the world, is truly remarkable for many reasons, not least the fact that it is no staid museum piece but still hosts classical and pop concerts regularly, weaving itself very much into the fabric of modern society. Thankfully, a bizarre plan by the Venetians in the 19th century to have it taken down stone by stone and shipped off to Venice was never realized. Open winter 09:00–17:00, summer 08:00–20:00.

Below: *Pula's Roman Amphitheatre is still being used as an open-air venue today.*

Roman Pula ★★

Pula's Roman remnants do not end with the amphitheatre as you can easily follow their trail through the city with two of the original Roman town gates still standing. Head for the **Archaeological Museum**, which has a number of Roman artefacts including gravestones, and whose grounds feature a small arena that is used for concerts in summer, then make for the nearby **Triumphal Arch of Sergius**, which has been standing since 27BC when it was built by the local family of the same name.

A more recent slice of history lies close to the arch, with a sign denoting the house where the seminal Irish writer **James Joyce** once lived when he was teaching English in the city. From here continue on Sergijevaca and you will soon arrive at the old **Roman Forum**, which was once the centre of Roman life. The most impressive remains here are of the **Temple of Augustus**, which took a decade to build back in the 1st century AD and still sports its mighty columns. Today it houses a collection of Roman artefacts and sculptures. Take a seat in one of the cafés on the square and you can admire it in all its glory.

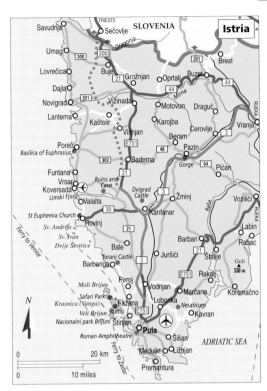

NORTH ALONG THE COAST TO ROVINJ
Mummies of Vodjnan **

If you have a taste for the macabre or just fancy a day trip with a difference, head out of Pula on the road towards Rovinj and make for the sleepy village of Vodjnan. The disproportionately large **Church of St Blaise** is as tall as St Mark's Basilica in Venice and it harbours a spooky secret. Behind the main altar are the preserved corpses of **St Nikolosa Bursa**, **St Giovanni Olini** and **St Leon Bembo**. The story behind Bembo is that he shunned the decadent life and glory of the Divine Republic and left Venice forever to eke out a simple and pious life instead. The church is popular with pilgrims who claim it has divine powers, and they

ON TO SLOVENIA

The Venetian-style town of Piran, on Slovenia's Adriatic coast, is an easy day trip from Istria, with direct buses running there from Poreč and Pula. Those with more time may want to head further afield to one of Europe's most charming small capital cities, Ljubljana (neatly divided by its river into an old Baroque core and an Art Nouveau district), or to the alpine lakes of Bled and Bohinj.

Above: *The façade and bell tower of St Euphemia church in Rovinj.*

often point to the well-preserved mummies as proof. Open Mon–Sat 09:00–19:00.

Rovinj ★★★

The most striking town on the Istrian coastline is undoubtedly Rovinj, a spectacular Italianate gem jutting out atop a rocky outcrop in a collage of orange tiled roofs and dreamy church spires. Rovinj was once under Italian control and a legacy remains. Many locals are bilingual and a string of restaurants offers an array of Italian delights at very affordable prices. Over the last few decades a colony of artists has moved into Rovinj and the town now overflows with niche galleries, where the artists themselves are only too keen to talk about their work. Then there are the boutique shops where visitors can stock up on the fine local truffles, wines and other Epicurean treats.

Church of St Euphemia ★★

Istria's highest bell tower dominates Rovinj's skyline and sits atop this fine church, the present incarnation of which dates back to the 18th century. On the pinnacle of the bell tower is a statue of St Euphemia. Myths and legends surround the church. Perhaps the most intriguing is the story of how the sarcophagus of St Euphemia – who is said to have been thrown to the lions by Emperor Diocletian – came to rest in the church. It mysteriously washed ashore after a violent storm in the 9th century and the locals were stymied about how to heft its enormous bulk up the steep hillside.

Eventually a small boy appeared with his two cows after receiving a divine calling and achieved the impossible by spiriting her remains up the hillside. The sarcophagus of the town's patron saint remains inside the church on the hill overlooking to the town to this day. A touching more recent arrival is the wooden altar, built by refugee craftsman from the town of Vukovar, which was savaged by Serb attacks in the war of independence. Open daily 10:00–12:00, 16:00–19:00.

Grisia **

The winding stone street that curls from the Church of St Euphemia back down to the sea has been populated in recent years by small shops and galleries. Here you can pick up everything from painted seashells and pearl necklaces, through to fresh truffles and local wines. There are some genuinely interesting works of art nestling among a horde of tourist souvenirs, making an hour or so rambling around nosing into the tiny shops a real pleasure. Note that most of the shops close completely in the depths of winter.

Rovinj Town Museum *

If your interest in Rovinj goes beyond its chocolate-box beauty, then make a beeline for the local civic museum. Some of the highlights include examples of local costumes through the ages and paintings dating from the 15th to the 19th centuries, as well as works by local Istrian painters. Perhaps the highlight is the 16th-century *Christ Crowned with Thorns* by Pietro Mera. Open Mon–Sat 09:30–12:30, 18:00–21:30.

Summer Nights in Rovinj **

In season, Rovinj is a delightful place to be. After a day at the beach or out on a boat things really come alive in town in the early evening as the locals take their posing promenades dressed up in their finest clothes. Then it is time for an alfresco meal in one of the numerous **seafood restaurants**, before indulging in some of the excellent **local ice cream** (*sladoled*), which any Italian would be proud of. Perhaps the

---

ISTRIAN TRUFFLES

These pungent fungi are traditionally harvested with pigs who sniff them out; today the pigs are being replaced by dogs, but black and white Istrian truffles (*tartufi*) remain on a par with those from Italy and France. The world's largest white truffle was discovered near the town of Livade, weighing 1.3kg (2.9lb). *Tartufi* (chopped, grated, ground and contained in oil) features on menus throughout Croatia and should not be missed.

Below: *The skyline of Rovinj Old Town overlooking the Adriatic.*

most sublime venue in Rovinj is **Valentino's Cocktail Bar**, where a cushion comes with your order to enable you to ease down onto the rocks and savour a dramatic Adriatic sunset.

Rovinj Aquarium *

Part of the **Ruđer Bošković Centre for Maritime Research**, this is a good place to visit on a rainy day, especially if you are interested in the local sea life and don't have time to dive or snorkel, or if you have kids in tow. The modest aquarium, one of the oldest in Europe, having opened in 1891, focuses on a variety of Adriatic marine life with the highlights dazzlingly colourful species and the poisonous scorpion fish. Open daily 09:00–20:00 in summer only.

UP THE COAST TO POREČ
Limski Fjord **

The nearest Croatia has to a fjord hides away just to the north of Rovinj and is easily accessible on a day trip from any of the coastal resort towns. It is well worth the detour from the main highway if you are driving, especially if you love seafood, as there are some great waterside restaurants which serve up the fresh produce that the fjord so abundantly provides including excellent oysters and mussels. Limski is a striking sight as it cuts a 9km (5-mile) deep swathe in from the Adriatic in a wash of emerald water and thick rock walls. This hidden spot is barely visible from the sea and once Adriatic pirates lurked in here awaiting ships to ambush. The **viewing gallery** high above the fjord on the road to Poreč is the best place to get a real feel for the beauty of the inlet and its tree shrouded setting.

Opposite: *The remarkable Basilica of Euphrasius in Poreč.*
Below: *Limski Fjord, just north of Rovinj.*

Vrsar *

Many people skip by the old fishing village of Vrsar in their rush to get to Poreč, but it is worth a lunch stop at least. There is a sprinkling of decent places in which to eat and plenty of cafés to relax in on a warm day and enjoy the Adriatic breezes. The architectural highlight is **St Martin's Church** (easily spotted thanks to its voluminous bell tower, only added in 1991), which is well worth popping into. Look out for the frescoes, quite striking despite the fact that they were only a post-World War II addition. The local castle houses a collection of art by seminal Croatian painter **Edo Mrtić**. Visitors keen to enjoy a naturist experience can dispense with their clothing at nearby **Koversada**, a large naturist resort that opened here as far back as the 1960s and is still very popular.

Poreč **

Poreč is the granddaddy of all the Croatian coastal resorts and is also home to one of the country's most remarkable historical attractions, the **Basilica of Euphrasius**. Tito planned to use resorts like this to draw in much-needed hard currency from tourists and it worked like a dream here with Poreč drawing in hundreds of thousands of visitors every year from all over Europe. The war of independence did dent tourism but didn't inflict any physical damage. Slowly numbers are climbing back up to postwar levels and this is once again a busy resort. It caters for holiday-makers' every need through the massive hotels of Zelena Laguna, as well as a flurry of cafés, bars, restaurants, water sports and day trip options. One of the biggest surprises to many visitors is that Poreč has a compelling old core, which contains a swathe of very well-preserved Roman streets.

Basilica of Euphrasius ***

The **UNESCO World Heritage** listed Basilica of St Euphrasius is truly mind-boggling. This is quite simply one of the finest examples of Byzantine art and architecture in existence and should not be missed. Unlike

LIGHTHOUSES

Those looking for a tranquil and secluded break can arrange to stay in one of 11 specially renovated lighthouses located in Istria and Dalmatia. Dramatic sea views, opportunities for fishing, diving, windsurfing and secluded walks are all part of the lighthouse attractions. Some of the accommodation is exclusive, while other lighthouses have been divided into two to four apartments, with the largest capacity of a single property being 16 people. Due to their popularity a minimum booking of a week is usually required. Further information is available from the Croatia National Tourist Board (www.croatia.hr) and also from Adriatica.net (http://adriatica.net).

MS DALMACIJA

One of the most pleasant ways to explore the Croatian coast is on board the three-star cruise ship, the *MS Dalmacija*, which operates a round trip to Venice, taking in Pula, Kotor (Montenegro), Dubrovnik, Korčula and Split en route. Currently the only cruise ship that travels along Croatia's coast, facilities on board are comfortable rather than luxurious.
Uljanik Shipmanagement Inc, Carrarina 6, 52100 Pula, tel: (052) 212-955, fax: (052) 221-339, website: www.cruiseadriatic.com

many ecclesiastical sights around the world there is no whacking entrance charge or limited opportunity for viewing. Here you can breeze in and admire this unique work of art as often as you like for free and get right up close as well.

The finest artists and craftsmen of the day were brought in during the 6th century from the likes of Ravenna and Constantinople to concoct this Byzantine dream, whose highlights are the frescoes in the apse, laden with sparkling gold and mother-of-pearl, as well as a treasure trove of precious and semi-precious stones. Look out also for the figure of St Euphrasius himself, proudly carrying a model of Poreč to the left of the main frescoes.

Away from the apse be sure to check out the even older **mosaics** near the main door that have been uncovered below floor level. These have been dated to as far back as the 4th century, giving an insight into the true antiquity of this special site. The best place to

take it all in is from the rather more modern (well, modern at least for the basilica as they date from the 15th century) wooden pews. For a good view over Poreč go back out of the basilica and take the stairs up the 16th-century bell tower. Open 07:00–20:00.

Roman Poreč **

On a crowded summer's day little in Poreč hints at its Roman past, but out of season or late at night you can wander down the old **Decamanus** thoroughfare, once smoothed by Roman sandals, and dream of days gone by. Many of the buildings along the street, and neighbouring **Eufrazijeva** (another Roman artery), are now lined by Venetian-style or modern buildings, but some Roman artefacts can be viewed around the old **Forum**, which is still being excavated. This was once the site of the temples of Mars and Neptune, but today little remains so you will have to let your imagination do the work.

Romanesque House *

This 13th-century concoction lies towards the southern end of Decamanus. In summer it is a delightful venue for **live music and cultural performances**. Inside is a **small art gallery** where you can also pick up souvenirs. The wooden balcony you may have noticed from further down the street, thinking it might make a good spot to survey the length of the Decamanus, is unfortunately not currently open to the public. Open daily10:00–12:00 and 18:00–20:00, summer only.

THE REST OF THE ISTRIAN COAST
Brijuni Islands **

This string of islands has a long history of human habitation, but perhaps the most famous resident of them all has been Tito. The Yugoslav leader liked nothing better than cruising down here to impress various visiting heads of state or indulge, allegedly, in a spot of extra-marital activity with a string of mistresses. The islands are now accessible on day trips from the Istrian resorts as well as from the coastal town of Fažana, though many of these are too shepherded and claustrophobic for more independent visitors. Another option is to stay the night at one of the hotels on the islands.

In total there are 14 islands in the **Brijuni Islands National Park**, which only became a protected haven rather than an out-and-out playground in 1983. Illustrious visitors apart from Tito (who, it is said, often spent half a year here) include **James Joyce, Thomas Mann, Nasser** and, somewhat controversially, terrorist **Abu Nidal**. Various dignitaries, including royalty and politicians, have also breezed through leaving a somewhat bizarre legacy. In the **Brijuni Safari Park** is a weird and wonderful collection of flora and fauna, including the likes of **llamas, giraffes** and **zebra**, presented to Tito by some of his famous guests.

JAMES JOYCE

In October 1904 the Irish writer James Joyce moved from Trieste to Pula. In the five short months that he lived in the city Joyce spent his time teaching English to Austro-Hungarian naval officers at the Berlitz language school. Capitalizing on the Joyce link, modern-day Pula boasts a memorial plaque dedicated to the writer and the Uliks (Ulysses) café-bar, where Mate Čuljak's bronze statue of the Dubliner reclines on the terrace.

Opposite: *The heart of Roman Poreč.*
Below: *A statue of Pula's one-time resident and writer, James Joyce.*

Other things to look out for on the two islands (visitors can only gain access to **Veli Brijun** and **Mali Brijun**) are the ruins of a **Byzantine castle** and a modest museum dedicated to Tito. One noted absentee from Brijuni these days is Štipe Mesic, the Croatian president who has shunned the retreat as a symbol of communist-era decadence, unlike his predecessor, Franjo Tuđman, who enjoyed relaxing here.

Above: *The ferry to the Brijun islands.*

Other Coastal Resorts *

As tourism picks back up again, the smaller resorts of **Novigrad** and **Umag** are starting to develop, with new hotels and revamped marinas to cater for one of the fastest growing sectors of Croatian tourism. Novigrad visually resembles Rovinj, with Venetian architectural touches and a landmark bell tower, albeit on a smaller scale. Though some of its charm has been tainted by untidy hotel development, it is worth popping into, especially if you like seafood, as there are some good restaurants. Umag, meanwhile, is another growing resort with a small population that rises to prominence once a year when it holds an ATP event, the Croatian Tennis Open. There are a number of hotels in and around town but sadly no real beaches, so lovers of concrete bathing platforms will be in heaven.

INLAND ISTRIA

Delve in from the shiny resorts of the Adriatic coast and the roads soon climb up into an altogether less developed world of vine-shrouded slopes, rolling hills (many of which offer impressive views back towards the sea), lush forests and chocolate-box-pretty hill towns. The likes of **Motovun**, **Grožnjan** and **Vižinada** seem to belong to a different age, with their clanging church bells and crumbling old streets. Here, little shops selling local produce rather than supermarkets are the norm.

The regional tourist authorities have finally discovered the potential of the hinterland and have now set up the **Istria County Tourism Association** with the aim of promoting rural small-scale ecotourism. The Association already has over 180 members who among them have created around 1500 beds as part of their 'agroturizam' drive. Here you can stay in old farmhouses in the hills and enjoy simply cooked food that often includes gastronomic treats like fresh truffles shaved over scrambled eggs.

Truffles (*see* panel, page 73) are indigenous to the forests of Istria. The story goes that they were discovered by an Italian soldier who, when he was stationed in Istria, suspected there might be truffles in the area. He later returned with his dogs to hunt for the delicacy. You can find truffles from the hinterland on restaurant menus throughout Istria as a whole.

You really need a car to get up and around inland Istria, but if you are staying in the area for a few days there are plenty of opportunities for **walking** and **cycling** on numerous trails. One of the most interesting routes is the 27km (17-mile) trail on an old wine railway route from Vižinada to the village of Kaštelir. Check with the local tourist offices in the resort towns before you strike out and you can embark on cycling and walking adventures on trails that link the villages, taking in swathes of stunning scenery on the way.

Motovun ★★

Motovun is one of the most visited of all the hill towns and with good reason as from afar it is perhaps the most striking. It rests 280m (750ft) above sea level, dominating

---

CROATIA'S OLDEST WINE REGION

Istria's wine-growing tradition dates back to the time of ancient Greece. Locals claim the name Kalovinja Bay is derived from the Greek word for good wine. Istrian wine was also popular with the Romans, the Venetians and the Habsburgs. Today wine is grown in central, eastern and western Istria, the latter region having the biggest concentration of vineyards.

Below: *Typical charming Inland Istrian hill town.*

the surrounding vineyards and forests of the Mirna valley. The drive here is all part of the fun as the road winds up around the steep hillside trying to sneak into the once heavily fortified town. The sturdy old town walls still remain but the welcome for today's visitors is far friendlier that that meted out to marauding pirates who once threatened the towns of inland Istria. Motovun also welcomes artists, with a few **galleries and studios** opening their doors to visitors during the summer months. Since 1999 this emerging cultural destination has staged its own annual film festival in the summer months.

Once inside the walls, the stamp of Venice is immediately apparent as you will find the trademark lion carved into many buildings around town. Architecturally the few modern buildings are overshadowed by Gothic, Venetian, Renaissance and Romanesque creations, the highlight of which is **St Stephen's Church**. This Renaissance parish church was designed by a Venetian architect in the 17th century. View the marble statues of **St Lawrence** and **St Stephen** on the altar and, if it is open, hike up the stairs of the bell tower (or stroll around the town walls) for some memorable views of this unforgettable region.

Below: *The dramatic old core of Vižinada.*

Vižinada *

If you want to feel as if you have chanced upon your own little hill town then pop into Vižinada for a few hours. This tiny little village manages to sneak in a few **Roman** and **Venetians remnants** but no tourist facilities, with only one café and one restaurant in a village where the locals appear genuinely surprised to see you. As more and more people explore the hinterland and snap up properties, places like Vižinada won't exist for much longer. The old town square has a crumble of old churches as well as a few Roman bits and pieces and a Venetian loggia, and the square makes an atmospheric venue for occasional concerts in the summer months.

Above: *Innovative art on sale in Inland Istria.*

Grožnjan ***

Grožnjan is perhaps the most charming of all the Istrian hill towns. It features the standard attractions of an old quarter set spectacularly on its own lofty bluff, with orange roof-tiled houses crowding around a small church, but it has much more to offer. After Italian immigrants fled the new socialist state after World War II, the town had fallen into a state of disrepair – that was until the authorities coaxed **artists** and **artisans** in with the promise of free rents and help in renovating the dilapidated properties.

This foresight has been rewarded and now dozens of artists work within the old town and you can tour the various **workshops** and **galleries**, talking to the artists and buying directly from them rather than in a tourist shop. The esoteric creations on offer up here make truly unique souvenirs and help create an ambience that is further enhanced during the summer by the **Jeunesses Musicales Croatia** (a youth music school) which sets up house in the old town. As you stroll around pondering what to buy, your spirits are lifted further by the strains of a violin or a sweet voice as you gaze out over the surrounding countryside below and congratulate yourself on making it up to Grožjnan.

Above: *Pazin's limestone gorge is its most striking geographical feature.*

Many of Grožjnan's ramble of old stone houses are attractive, but the most interesting buildings in town are the **Venetian-era loggia** as well as the **Church of St Vitus and St Modestus**, an 18th-century structure with its own bell tower.

Pazin ★

While it may not be as chocolate-box pretty as the trio above, Pazin has the feel of a real town and also boasts a few things to see. Only a 35km (22-mile) drive north of Poreč, Pazin was once the capital of Istria, but those glory days are firmly behind it. The most striking geographical feature of Pazin is the vertiginous **limestone gorge** that plunges over 100m (330ft) into the earth beneath the town. This gorge was said to have been the inspiration for Jules Verne in his novel *Matthias Sandorf* and the locals claim it was also seminal for Dante in his *Inferno*.

Elsewhere around town things to look for include the **Church of St Nicholas**, with a Romanesque main building and 18th-century bell tower. Inside are a series of interesting Gothic frescoes and the coat of arms of the town, the oldest of its kind left in Pazin today. **Pazin Castle**, a sturdy old fortress, is also worth popping into as it houses the **Ethnographic Museum of Istria**. On display are traditional costumes from various periods, exhibits covering fishing on the coast and farming in the interior as well as the fruits of local archaeological digs. The castle is also a venue for various cultural shows, live music and temporary exhibitions.

Beram ★★★

A short 5km (3-mile) drive from Pazin is the sleepy village of Beram. The main reason to visit is to view the remarkable **15th-century frescoes** in the **Church of St Mary**. You may need to ask around the village to get the key, but the effort is well worth it. The series covers the life of the Virgin Mary and the story of Adam and

Eve, but the most dramatic frescoes depict the *Dance of Death* in chilling fashion. The scenes are all set with an Istrian backdrop, making them useful as an anthropological and historic study as well as an artistic and ecclesiastical one.

Istrian Wine Road ★★★

The proactive Istria County Tourist Association has produced an English-language guide to Istria's bountiful wine roads. For years local families have headed inland at weekends to stock up on the excellent wines (wine has been produced here since at least Roman times). Three main routes are depicted (Buje, Buzet and Poreč), with plenty of recommendations on specific vineyards to visit, many of them offering tastings. Most of the vineyards are located north of Poreč en route to the Slovenian border and are easy enough to get to if you have your own wheels, since public transport is patchy at best. The prices and quality vary immensely, ranging from 20 kuna for a simple bottle of Malvazija white wine through to over 100 kuna for a decent Teran red. The leaflet is available free of charge from local tourist offices throughout the region, but even if you cannot get hold of it you can still meander off into the countryside to explore the vineyards for yourself.

NIGHTLY FASHION PARADE

Croatians and visiting Italians make an effort to look their best at night in Istria's coastal resorts, with many donning their trendiest clothes simply to go for a walk, or to look cool hanging around the waterfront. While you don't need to go to these lengths, bars and nightclubs tend to attract a crowd that dresses to impress, so bring your favourite clubbing outfit if you are intending to party.

Below: *Inland Istria – a region of vineyards and rolling hills.*

Istria at a Glance

BEST TIMES TO VISIT

Despite its idyllic weather, with year-round sunshine, hot summer days, warm springs and autumns and mild winters, Istria has a definite off-season. From Nov–Apr the majority of restaurants, cafés and bars are closed, due to the lack of tourist demand. Camping is also out at this time of year, although those seeking a tranquil break will still find somewhere to stay and eat. The off-peak seasons (**Apr–Jun** and **Sep–Oct**) are the best months to visit with all tourist facilities open, but less demand placed on them.

GETTING THERE

By Air: Charter flights from around Europe land at Pula airport in summer. Croatia Airlines also operate domestic services to Pula from Zagreb, Split and Dubrovnik.
By Rail: Pula has a station; direct services are limited.
By Road: Istria is accessible by road from the Kvarner Gulf region of Croatia, Slovenia and Trieste. Pula is the region's main bus terminal; domestic services arrive and depart from Zagreb and Dubrovnik. Buses run from other Dalmatian towns and cities, as well as Rijeka and Opatija in the Kvarner Gulf. Many buses also stop in Poreč and Rovinj.
By Boat: Marinas along the Istrian coast have plenty of mooring spaces for yachts; Pula is becoming a popular

stop on the cruise ship circuit. There is a limited ferry service between Pula and Zadar. The Brujini Islands are only accessible by boat, with services leaving from Fažana and Pula.

GETTING AROUND

Pula, Poreč, Rovinj, Umag and Novigrad all have city bus services, but tourists have limited call to use them. A single bus service links all these destinations. Taxis are readily available in the popular tourist areas. You'll need a car to explore Motovun and Grožnjan in Inland Istria.

WHERE TO STAY

Pula
MID-RANGE
Hotel Valsabbion, Pješèana Ulva IX/26, tel: 052 218 033, fax: 052 218 033, www.valsabion.com Design hotel on the waterfront near Pula's Veruda Marina. It also has a swimming pool, small fitness centre and an aerobics studio.

BUDGET
Hotel Riviera, Splitska 1, tel: 052 211 166, fax: 052 219 117, www.arenaturist.hr A functional but centrally located hotel housed in an attractive Viennese Villa.
Pula Youth Hostel, Zaljev Valsaline 4, tel: 052 391 133, fax: 052 391 106. Beachfront hostel overlooking the attractive Valsaline Bay just a short journey from the city centre. Take bus numbers 2 or 3.

Poreč
MID-RANGE
Neptun, Maršala Tita, tel: 052 400 800, fax: 052 431 351, www.riviera.hr The best of Poreč's central hotels.

Rovinj
LUXURY
Hotel Villa Angelo D'oro, Via Svalba 38-42, tel: 052 840 502, fax: 052 840 112, www.rovinj.at Classical elegance pervades at this 17th-century palace-cum-boutique hotel.

MID-RANGE
Hotel Adriatic, P. Budicin bb, tel: 052 815 088, fax: 052 813 573, www.adriaresorts.hr Charming hotel overlooking the main square.

BUDGET
Hotel Rovinj, Sv. Križa 59, tel: 052 811 288, fax: 052 840 757. Superb elevated location overlooking the sea and near a concrete beach. Rooms are simply furnished but some have balconies offering great views.

Umag
LUXURY
Hotel Kristal Obala, J. B. Tita 9, tel: 052 700 000, fax: 052 700 499, www.hotel-kristal.com Easy-to-find hotel, pink exterior; comfortable rooms with balconies overlooking the sea. A great location near the marina in the older part of town. Large outdoor pool and onsite restaurant.

Istria at a Glance

Brijuni Islands
LUXURY
Hotel Karmen, Veli Brijuni, tel: 052 525 400, fax: 052 212 110. Stay in the shadow of Marshall Tito.

Novigrad
MID-RANGE
Hotel Cittar, Cittanova, tel: 052 757 735, fax: 052 757 340, www.cittar.hr Family-run hotel in the heart of town.

Inland Istria
MID-RANGE
Hotel Kaštel, Trg Andrea Antičo, Motovun, tel: 052 681 607, fax: 052 681 652, www.hotel-kastel-motovun.hr Housed in a former 17th-century palace; all the rooms have commanding views.

WHERE TO EAT

Pula
Restaurant Valsabbion (see Hotel Valsabbion). Innovative Istrian cuisine and unique serving more than justify the restaurant's multiple awards. In summer reserve a terrace seat overlooking the marina.

Poreč
Sofora, Maršala Tita 13, tel: 052 432 053. Waterfront restaurant serving hearty and affordable Croatian staples. The fresh seafood is great.

Rovinj
Al Gastaldo, Iza Kasarne 14, tel: 052 814 109. First-rate Istrian food and a good-value wine list are hard to beat. Have a dish with truffles every time.

Umag
Restoran Allegro, (see Hotel Kristal). Enjoy seafood dishes on the outdoor terrace.

Novigrad
Mandrać, Mandrać 6, tel: 052 757 120. Renowned for its fresh fish and harbour views.

Grožnjan
Caffe Bar Arta, Trg Cornesa, tel: 052 776 405. Stunning views, late opening hours.

Motovun
Hotel Kaštel (see Where to Stay). Savour Istrian fare on the hotel's leafy terrace. Dine inside during winter.

SHOPPING

Istria is a great place to stock up on Croatian souvenirs. For original artwork try Rovinj's **Ulica Grisia**; more standard tourist fare abounds on Poreč's main thoroughfare, **Ulica Decamanus**. Numerous outlets of the **Zigante Tartufi** stores sell wine, olive oil and other Croatian produce, as well as the hallowed truffle.

EXCURSIONS

You can join a 40-minute walk through the **Jama Baredine** (Baredine Cave) which has some impressive stalagmites and stalactites; tel: 052 421 333.

USEFUL CONTACTS

Pula Tourist Information, Forum 3, tel: 052 219 197, www.gradpula.com/tourist
Pula Airport, Valtursko Polje, tel: 052 550 0900
Zigante Tartufi, Smareglina 5, tel: 052 214 855, www.zigantetartufi.com
Poreč Tourist Information, Zagrebačka 9, tel: 052 451 293, fax: 052 451 665, www.istra.com/porec
Rovinj Tourist Information, Pina Budičina 12, tel: 052 811 566, fax: 052 816 007, www.tzgrovinj.hr
Umag, Trgovačka 6, tel: 052 741 363, fax: 052 741 649, www.istra.com/umag
Novigrad, Porporella 1, p.p. 52, tel: 052 757 075, www.istra.com/novigrad
Grožnjan Tourist Information, Umberta Gorjana 3, tel: 052 776 131, www.groznjan-grisignana.hr
Motovun Tourist Information, Šetaliste V. Nazora 1, tel: 052 681 642, fax: 052 681 642.

PULA	J	F	M	A	M	J	J	A	S	O	N	D
AVERAGE TEMP. °C	5	5	8	11	15	19	22	22	18	15	9	6
AVERAGE TEMP. °F	41	42	47	52	60	67	73	72	66	54	49	44
HOURS OF SUN DAILY	3.9	4.7	5.4	6.6	7.9	8.9	10.3	9.4	7.8	5.9	3.7	3.4
RAINFALL mm	70	60	60	70	50	50	40	70	80	70	110	80
RAINFALL in	3.1	2.5	2.5	2.8	2.2	2.1	1.9	3.0	3.4	3.1	4.4	3.3
DAYS OF RAINFALL	9	8	8	8	7	6	4	7	8	8	10	9

6
Kvarner Gulf

While Dalmatia and Istria glisten as Croatia's coastal tourist stars the Kvarner Gulf remains relatively unheralded with no direct scheduled international flights into the region and less tourist development on the whole. This is certainly not due to a lack of attractions or scenic splendour. This compelling region, set around the shores of the sweeping Kvarner Gulf, abounds with islands, mountain ranges and beaches.

The main city of **Rijeka** may not have Zagreb's sophistication or Split's buzz, but it is worth more than the ferry stopover most people spare it. A short drive to the northwest is the **Opatija Riviera**, an oasis whose temperate climate has made it a popular and chic retreat for over a century. South along the coast from Rijeka the Adriatic Highway squeezes between the shimmering Adriatic and the hulking fortress-like limestone walls of the **Velebit Mountains**, which are perfect for climbing and hiking.

Offshore the Kvarner Gulf tempts with its sprinkling of islands. The most popular, perhaps partly as it is connected by a bridge to the mainland, is **Krk**, with its busy resorts. **Rab** also gets many tourists and **Rab Town** is one of Croatia's most stunning coastal towns. More and more visitors are starting to discover the charms of **Cres**, **Veli Lošinj**, **Mali Lošinj** and **Pag**, the latter strikingly barren and renowned for producing Croatia's most revered cheese, as well as being a centre for traditional lace production.

DON'T MISS

*** Trsat, Rijeka: head up here for sweeping views over the Kvarner Gulf.
*** Opatija: step back in time to this charming and relaxed 19th-century resort.
*** Paklenica National Park: Mountain oasis for walkers, hikers and climbers.
*** Rab Town: picture-perfect Old Town with dreamy church spires.
** Baška: popular but low-key beach resort, stunning views of the Velebit Mountains.
** Pag: eerily barren island renowned for the quality of its cheese, lamb and lace.

Opposite: *View of the Velebit Mountains.*

RIJEKA

Rijeka, with over 160,000 inhabitants, is the only city in the Kvarner Gulf and is also one of Croatia's busiest ports. People often pass through without giving it more than a second glance, but it is worth at least a day if not an overnight stay. The port is as untidy and rambling as most and the city is blighted by a string of ugly high-rise suburbs, but the core has a graceful Austro-Hungarian appearance that no other city on the Croatian coast can boast. The city's golden age may have been when the rail lines from Vienna and Budapest converged here for access to the port in the 19th century, but the city is on the rise again as its harbour has the advantage over Adriatic competitors like Koper and Trieste since its water is deeper.

Korzo *

Rijeka's main street overflows with lavish 18th- and 19th-century buildings that give it the feel of a provincial town in Austria rather than a Mediterranean port. Despite a ramble of fast-food restaurants and shops the grand designs can still be seen. The 18th-century **City Tower** is the street's most dramatic building, easily identifiable thanks to its quartet of clocks and the Austro-Hungarian eagle that recalls the days when Croatia was far from independent.

Rijeka

Old Town *

There have been some moves to revamp Rijeka's small old quarter, which lies just north of the Korzo, but much of it is still quite shabby. The main space here is **Trg Ivana Koblera**, which is home to an interesting piece of modern sculpture by indigenous artist **Igor Emilio**. Nearby is the **Roman Arch**, an indication that Rijeka's history goes back a lot further than the arrival of the Austro-Hungarians. Another short walk brings you to the **Church of St Vitus**, the centre's most interesting church. The cylindrical main part of the design is fronted by a neoclassical façade. Be careful not to blaspheme inside as local legend has it that one dissenter who hurled a stone at the Gothic crucifix paid the price when the ground instantly swallowed him up.

Above: *Old Rijeka with its modern suburbs in the background.*

Parks and Museums **

If you are looking for a green space to escape the city, continue north from the Old Town and you will soon come to **Park Nikole Hosta**, which houses the **City Museum**, the **Naval and Maritime Museum** and the **Natural History Museum**. The **City Museum** in communist times had the grand moniker of the 'Museum of National Revolution', though these days this is not exactly a grand place. There are some interesting artefacts from local archaeological digs, including remnants of the days when Rijeka was the Roman city of Tarsatica. Open Mon–Fri 17:00–20:00, Sat 10:00–13:00.

The **Naval and Maritime Museum**, linked to the City Museum by an arcade dotted with a few sculptures, occupies the far more impressive former palace of the governor of Rijeka. There is all sorts of maritime bric-a-brac, from models of Rijeka-built tankers and grainy black and white photos through to stuffed sharks and weapons. Rijeka claims to have been the birthplace of the torpedo, invented by local man Ivan Lupis in 1878, and there are torpedo-firing cannons on show in the museum. Open Tue–Sat 09:00–13:00.

The **Natural History Museum** has taken over an attractive 19th-century building and put on display a host of Adriatic marine life and fauna. There is a

GLAGOLITIC SCRIPT

In the 9th century two monks, Cyril and Methodus, set about converting the Slavs to Christianity and developed a new alphabet to help them do so. This 38-letter alphabet was adopted by Croatian priests and became increasingly widespread, with some members of the clergy using it until the 19th century. Austrian attempts to ban the use of Glagolitic had the opposite effect and indeed prompted many to use what they came to define as a Croatian written language.

modest aquarium, with all sorts of indigenous species, as well as a display of rocks and fossils showing how life developed in the Adriatic over the centuries. A more recent addition has been a multimedia presentation. Open Mon–Fri 09:00–19:00.

Trsat ***

This hilly hideaway high above the city is Rijeka's must-see attraction. The **views** are impressive – sweeping out across the city, taking in the slopes of Mount Učka and on towards the islands of the Kvarner Gulf. It is a steep 561-step climb up, but thankfully there is also a public bus service. There has been a **fortress** here since long before the arrival of the Romans when Illyrian tribes held sway over the region. Much of what you see dates back to the 13th century and the Frankopan era, though work to bring it back to its full glory is ongoing. The sturdy walls and superstructure have been patched up enough to allow **cultural performances** and **live music** in summer.

Church of Our Lady of Trsat **

Just back from the castle is one of Croatia's most important churches, the **Church of Our Lady of Trsat**. Pious citizens of Rijeka insist that the Virgin Mary came to stay here after fleeing Nazareth before continuing on to Italy. The interior of the church is festooned with various pleas for divine intervention, messages of thanks and other religious paraphernalia.

Below: *The waterfront of the resort at Opatija.*

OPATIJA RIVIERA

The Opatija Riviera, stretching for 40km (25 miles) along the western fringes of the Kvarner Gulf, has been a playground for Europe's well-heeled classes since the 19th century when the citizens of Vienna and Budapest flocked to enjoy the famed balmy microclimate and eat their *Sachertorte* by the sea. The area declined under communist rule, but in the last decade has undergone something of a renaissance, with its grand 19th-century hotels brought back to their opulent best, allowing an older demographic to enjoy its sedate charms.

Opatija ★★★

The first hotel in Opatija, the Kvarner Hotel, opened as far back as 1885, taking advantage of the new rail connection to Rijeka from Vienna and Budapest. Soon the growing resort sported lavish hotels, waterfront promenades and sumptuous gardens where Europe's moneyed classes came to recline and enjoy health treatments or just the climate, which is said to be beneficial for a range of conditions, ranging from lung problems through to stress. The grand hotels themselves are really the big attractions as they strut proudly by the waterfront in all their refurbished glory. Staying in the Kvarner Hotel or the Millennium allows visitors to enjoy their own slice of 19th-century living.

Above: *The Millenium Hotel in the resort of Opatija.*

Lovran and Volosko ★★

The *lungomare* promenade runs for 12km (7 miles) and connects the main resort of Opatija with the fishing village of Volosko to the north and the resort of Lovran to the south. **Lovran** is a smaller version of Opatija with a sprinkling of hotels, cafés and restaurants. It also provides a good starting point for a hike up mighty **Mount Učka**, a four-hour ascent that opens up remarkable views across the expanse of the Kvarner Gulf. The Učka range spreads its tentacles for 20km (12 miles) and there are mountain huts and trails for those wishing to spend more time up here, though advance planning and all the necessary equipment and provisions are necessary as this is a real mountain range with all the inherent dangers (and rewards).

Volosko meanwhile makes a good day trip as you can wander along the *lungomare* and then relax in the

GRIFFON VULTURES

At one time griffon vultures nested all over Croatia's Kvarner Gulf, yet their population fell into a rapid, and species-threatening decline as sheep farming and subsequently one of their main sources of food petered out. By the 1980s the situation had become critical and conservationists stepped in, teaching the locals to leave dead animals for the vultures and educating them about the environmental threats posed to the birds. Two decades on, the number of nesting birds on the island of Cres has increased threefold to over 150.

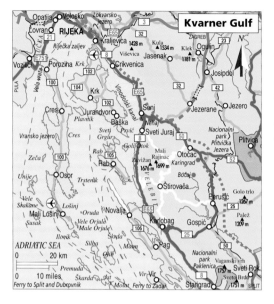

village over lunch. On a summer's day sitting in an alfresco restaurant enjoying fresh seafood is an extremely pleasant experience. Volosko no longer buzzes with the machinations of the busy local tuna fleet, but it is still a charming place to while away a few hours before strolling around the Adriatic back to Opatija or catching a bus back to Rijeka.

DOWN THE KVARNER GULF COAST

Most people bullet down the Adriatic Highway either to one of the islands or to Dalmatia, but it is worth stopping off to take in the unique history of **Senj** and the **Paklenica National Park**. The drive itself is spectacular with the **Velebit Mountains** on one side and the Adriatic on the other.

Senj *

Centuries ago the small coastal town of Senj was feared all around the Adriatic as it was home to fierce Uskok pirates. These fearsome maritime marauders furrowed the seas between modern-day Slovenia and Croatia, terrorizing passing trade and stamping on the toes of all the larger regional powers, especially the Ottomans against whom the Uskoks had a major grudge as they held them responsible for kicking them out of the interior before their arrival on the coast. Their power base in Senj was centred around the sturdy **Nehaj Fortress**. Eventually their power was reined in and, after the Treaty of Madrid in 1615, their fleets were disbanded as their Golden Age came to an end. Today they are remembered both by their fort (which houses an excellent museum that highlights their exploits) and also by an **annual festival** in August.

Paklenica National Park ***

The Paklenica National Park was set up just after World War II and today is an oasis for walkers, hikers and climbers. If you plan on staying over and don't want to hike up to one of the mountain huts, the best base is the modest town of **Starigrad** which offers a handful of cafés, restaurants and places to stay.

The park itself is just to the north and you can park right at the entrance where an entry fee is payable. It is a spectacular place; narrow gorges lead into a wilderness of towering rock walls crowned by sky-splitting peaks. From the top of the range the view is breathtaking as mountains loom all around and the islands of the Kvarner Gulf dot the distance. The park is split into two main sections of the Velebit Mountains: **Velika Paklenica** (big) and **Mala Paklenica** (small). Velika is the most user-friendly section with well-marked trails making it easy to navigate, while Mala is a bit rougher around the edges and a favourite with those wishing to get away from it all.

As you enter the park, look out for the shadowy **caves** that were off-limits during Yugoslav times as they were used as **secret bunkers** by the military. One of the great things about Paklenica is that it has something for every outdoors type, whether you simply want to stroll beside a mountain stream and take in the rejuvenating smell of the forests, head off for a few days in the real mountains, or even indulge in a spot of high-adrenaline free climbing (some routes have an X+ rating). Whatever you choose, don't underestimate Paklenica as the weather can change in minutes and what starts as a lovely bright summer's day can end in a violent thunderstorm.

HIKING IN PAKLENICA

Paklenica National Park offers hikers over 150km (93 miles) of trails ranging from relatively easy two-hour walks to those that take a number of days. Mountain huts along the route offer shelter to walkers, but due to space limitations should be booked in advance. The park administration publishes its own map of walking trails, which can be picked up from the office in the main car park.

Below: *A walking trail in Velika Paklenica.*

BLUE FLAG BEACHES

On the whole, Croatia's beaches and the sea surrounding them are very clean, with Blue Flag beaches dotted along the coast. The Kvarner Gulf alone has at least 19 Blue Flag beaches, with 41 more in Istria and 16 in Dalmatia. If you are looking for a Blue Flag beach in the Kvarner Gulf then head to the islands of Krk, Rab and Mali Lošinj.

ISLANDS

Krk *

Croatia's largest island is very popular with tourists, unsurprising really as it has a bridge from the mainland that makes it easy for Croats, Slovenes, Germans and Austrians as well as citizens from the former Soviet Bloc to breeze down for a Mediterranean holiday, and it is also home to Rijeka's airport.

Krk Town itself is no mere resort – it has a rambling old town laden with churches, fortified walls and old stone houses. **Krk Cathedral** is the top sight, with a 15th-century Frankopan chapel and an adjoining art gallery. Elsewhere around town look out for the **Canon's House** with an example of Glagolithic Script, the **Decamanus Art Gallery** with its Croatian domestic art, and the **Church of Our Lady**.

Baška **

Unless you are staying in them most of Krk's resorts have little appeal, though Baška stands out. The long **beach** here has won awards for its cleanliness and it boasts views out back to the Velebit Mountains and over to the neighbouring island of Rab; the resort itself has an appealing old quarter. This is a great place just to switch your brain off and relax for a few days, with a string of cafés, restaurants and bars on hand to help you, though this is by no means as brash and big a resort as you find in countries like Spain and Portugal.

Just a few miles from the town of Baška is the village of **Jurandvor**, home of **St Lucy's Church**. This was where the original **Baška Tablet** (see page 33), the earliest surviving example of Glagolitic Script, was found. However, the tablet on show

Below: *The popular resort of Baška on the island of Krk.*

here is a copy as the original has been taken off to be displayed in Zagreb.

Rab ***

Rab is most people's favourite Kvarner Gulf island. Development around much of the island has been kept to a minimum compared to Krk, and the capital vies with Korčula Town, Dubrovnik and Trogir for the title of Croatia's most attractive coastal settlement.

Rab Town has a wealth of church spires and winding stone streets on its own peninsula. You can bathe in the crystal-clear sea water whil staring up at the spires of the **Cathedral of St Mary the Great** and its 25m (82ft) high bell tower. Alternatively climb the tower and enjoy views of Rab Town and the Adriatic licking its fringes all around. Take a walk along Gornja Ulica and you can explore the **Church of St John**, the **Museum of Church Art**, the **Church of St Andrew** and, of course, the cathedral itself, which is home to a fine *Pieta* by the Dalmatian artist Petar and an interesting relief of Christ.

Above: *A small marina in Rab Town.*

In summer Rab Town buzzes with life and its restaurants are completely packed. At night the bars are also stuffed and the streets filled with tourists and locals taking a promenade in one of the most romantic old towns in Europe. By day there are numerous day-tour options, whether it be heading out for a cruise or exploring the rest of the island.

Pag **

The dry and barren island of Pag may not look too appealing, but it is worth coming here for the cheese alone. This is the home of the famous eponymous **sheep's cheese** you can find on restaurant menus all over the country. The island is also renowned for the high quality of its lace which is still produced by the local women and is increasingly sold to tourists. **Pag Town** itself may not be as striking as Rab Town, but it is

CROATIA'S IBIZA

The arid island of Pag is an unlikely location for some of Croatia's hottest nightlife, but during the summer Novalija's Zrće beach (a Blue Flag holder) is transformed into an Ibiza-style paradise. Join the locals and Croatian holiday-makers as they sip cocktails outside the Aquarius, Papaya and Calypso bar-clubs. Buses run from the town to the beach in high season.

a pleasant enough place to stay for a night or two and indulge in some of that sublime cheese.

Cres *

Clearly visible from the Opatija Riviera, the expansive but narrow island of Cres can be reached by ferry from Istria and Krk. The island is swathed in legends, not least that of **Jason and the Argonauts** who supposedly came here in their epic search for the Golden Fleece. Today it is one of Croatia's quieter islands, though its active fishing fleet makes it a good place to go if you like **seafood**, and it is also renowned for the high quality of its local lamb. The main town, **Cres Town**, has a decent choice of restaurants and also a **Franciscan Monastery**, **Venetian loggia** and the **Church of St Mary**, with its relief of the *Madonna and Child*.

Lošinj *

Just south across a narrow artificial channel from Cres is Lošinj. Its main resort of **Mali Lošinj** is an increasingly popular resort town and one of the most charming in the Kvarner Gulf. In season a litter of stalls curl around the deep harbour offering everything from fresh lavender and handicrafts to fruit and vegetables. Some of the **market stalls** are actually on boats, which bob prettily around the harbour. Elsewhere around town there is the 15th-century **Church of St Martin**, the Baroque **Church of the Virgin**, a couple of small **art galleries**, as well as plenty of **alfresco restaurants**.

Right: *The typically arid landscape of Pag.*

Kvarner Gulf at a Glance

The Kvarner Gulf is blessed with idyllic **spring** and **autumn** temperatures. In summer the resorts can be hot and crowded. Hoteliers have been trying to extend the tourist season, bringing good accommodation rates and spa facilities to Opatija in winter.

By Rail: A direct service links Rijeka and Zagreb.
By Road: Buses serve Rijeka from all over Croatia.
By Boat: Ferries from Split, Dubrovnik and Bari in Italy, stop at Rijeka. The islands are served by Jadrolinija ferries.

Buses operate throughout the region; Rijeka is the main hub.

Opatija
LUXURY
Hotel Millennium, Maršala Tita 109, tel: 051 202 000, fax: 051 2020 020, www.ugohoteli.hr Sachertorte from Vienna sets the standard for luxury in the hotel.
Rijeka
LUXURY
Grand Hotel Bonavia, Dolac 4, tel: 051 357 100, fax: 051 335 969, www.bonavia.hr Old-world luxury and service in this modern, central hotel.
Krk
MID-RANGE
Corinthia Hotel, Emila Geistlicha 38, Baška, tel: 051

656 111, fax: 051 856 584, www.hotelibaska.hr Accommodation in a collection of resort hotels.
BUDGET
Krk Youth Hostel, Vinka Vitezića 32, Krk Town, tel: 051 220 212. Busy hostel with some coveted double rooms.
Rab
MID-RANGE
Hotel Imperial, Palit bb, tel: 051 724 522, fax: 051 724 126, www.imperial.hr Located in the city park, with modern rooms.
Pag
MID-RANGE
Hotel Restaurant Biser, Pero Jeliniae bb, tel: 023 611 333, fax: 023 611 444, www.hotel-biser.com Small hotel with balconies and sea views.
Starigrad
MID-RANGE
Hotel Alan, Franje Tuđmana 14, tel: 023 369 236, fax: 023 369 203, www.hotel-alan.hr Popular for its family rooms and camp site.

Krk
Bistro Funtana (see Corinthia Hotel). Affordable set menu

and daily specials.
Opatija
Restaurant Amfora, tel: 051 701 222. Enjoy a romantic dinner overlooking the Gulf.
Rab
Paradiso, S. Radića 2, tel: 051 771 109. Dine in this former Roman foyer.
Rijeka
AS-Centar, Trg Republike Hrvatske 2, tel: 051 212 148. Cheap and central café.
Stari Grad
Hotel Alan (see Where to Stay). Good for a sit-down meal.

Krk Town Tourist Information, Trg Bana Josip Jelačića 1, tel: 051 221 415, fax: 051 221 126, www.grad-krk.hr
Baška Tourist Information, Kralja Zvonimir 114, Krk, tel: 051 856 544, fax: 051 856 544, www.tz-baska.hr
Opatija Tourist Information, Nikole Tesle 2, tel: 051 271 310, www.opatija-tourism.hr
Rab Town Tourist Information, Donja Ulica 2, tel: 051 771 111, www.tzg-rab.hr
Rijeka Tourist Information, Uzarska 14, tel: 051 335 882, www.multilink.hr/tz-rijeka

RIJEKA	J	F	M	A	M	J	J	A	S	O	N	D
AVERAGE TEMP. °C	5	6	9	12	16	20	23	23	19	15	10	7
AVERAGE TEMP. °F	42	43	49	54	62	69	74	74	67	60	50	45
HOURS OF SUN DAILY	4.0	4.9	5.6	6.8	8.0	9.1	10.5	9.7	8.1	6.1	3.9	3.7
RAINFALL mm	134.9	114.3	104	110.7	102.4	110.8	82	100.2	153	175.7	183.4	154.2
RAINFALL in	5.3	4.5	4.1	4.4	4.0	4.4	3.2	3.9	6.5	6.9	7.2	6.1
DAYS OF RAINFALL	11	9.4	10.2	11.6	12.3	11.9	9.1	9.2	9.8	10.9	12.4	11.6

7
Dalmatia

Dalmatia boasts one of the most scenically dramatic and thrilling coastlines on the planet. This thin Adriatic coastal strip overflows with pretty towns, historic cities and both Roman and Venetian legacies, while offshore a liberal sprinkling of islands tempts the traveller. Increasingly popular with tourists, Dalmatia these days is a popular choice not only for sun and sea holidays, but also for those who are interested in culture, as well as for sailing enthusiasts, adventure sports junkies and, thanks to the excellent food and wine that many Italians flock over for every summer, savvy gastronomes.

Situated in the southern corner of Dalmatia is the medieval city of **Dubrovnik**, Bryon's much eulogized 'Pearl of the Adriatic', but there is plenty more on offer than this, such as the northern cities of **Zadar** and **Šibenik** backed up in central Dalmatia by **Split**, Croatia's second city, and also the UNESCO World Heritage listed city of **Trogir**.

With so many islands off the Dalmatian coast it is difficult to pick one, so it is hardly surprising that island hopping is becoming increasingly popular. The most visited ones include **Brač**, **Hvar** and **Korčula**, but then there are also other gems like faraway **Vis**, from where Italy is clearly visible on a good day, and green **Mljet**. In short, these days Dalmatia has something for everyone, even, despite the hordes descending here from all over Europe during the summer months, those wanting to really get away from it all.

DON'T MISS

*** Dubrovnik: quite simply the 'Pearl of the Adriatic'.
*** Korčula Town: picture-perfect Old Town located on its own peninsula.
*** Kornati National Park: an archipelago of beautiful islands, great for sailing.
*** Trogir: UNESCO World Heritage listed medieval city full of historic buildings.
*** Diocletian's Palace: impressive Roman palace in Split's Old Town.
*** Hvar Town: idyllic island with Venetian-era houses.
*** Biševo's Blue Cave: ethereal light display on the island of Vis.

Opposite: *The Old Town walls of Dubrovnik.*

CLIMATE

With a Mediterranean climate that brings hot, dry summers and mild winters there is really no bad time to visit Dalmatia. This said some people find the heat – averaging 25°C (77°F) – and the tourist crowds too much in Jul–Aug. Spring, when daytime temperatures average around 12°C (54°F), and the landscape is lush and green, can be the most agreeable season in Dalmatia. The low season (Oct–Mar) has the most rainfall.

NORTHERN DALMATIA
Zadar **

Zadar was once Dalmatia's most important and largest conurbation, but these days this city of 100,000 inhabitants sits firmly in the shadow of Split and, in spite of its wealth of historic attractions and a dramatic setting, attracts surprisingly few visitors. During World War II Zadar was repeatedly bombed and then during the war of independence it was shelled on and off for the best part of four years. Only now, just over a decade on, is it starting to rediscover its legendary buzz. The old core sits proudly atop its own peninsula; enter through the Main Gate and slip back through the centuries.

Zadar's Forum **

Follow **Široka** and you will soon come to Zadar's most important historical buildings, all handily wrapped around the old **Roman Forum**. Give the **Pillar of Shame** a wide berth as this is traditionally where wrongdoers were brought to be publicly punished, a practice that ceased only as late as the mid-19th century. **St Donat's Church** is the standout here, a sturdy cylindrical structure that dates back to the 9th century. Commissioned by the Irish saint, the structure is a striking piece of Croatian sacral architecture, and like nothing else in the country. The church's stark interior is only brought to its best during classical recitals, which breathe life back into a building that no longer performs regular ecclesiastical duties. Look out for the Roman script on some of the stones that make up the church – these would originally have been part of the Roman Forum complex, and.are a testament to the victory of Christianity over the Romans.

Below: The old Venetian-era gate guarding the entrance to Zadar's Old Town.

Adjacent to St Donat's is a more active ecclesiastical structure, the **Cathedral of St Anastasia**, a largely Romanesque building with roots in the 12th century. The tomb of the saint herself lies within the walls and a stairway also leads up the bell tower for vertigo-defying views of the city and out towards the Adriatic islands. Across the Forum, much of it a messy expanse with a mash of old Roman columns and parked cars, is the rather unsightly looking **Archaeological Museum**. Various artefacts are on display that have been dredged up from the city's Neolithic, Roman and early Croatian history. Look out also for the Liburnian gravestones.

Zadar Archipelago ★★

Stretching out from the coastline of Zadar is a string of islands, such as **Molat**, **Ugljan** and **Pašman**, that are collectively known as the **Zadar Archipelago**. Many of them are still fairly unspoilt, although the largest, **Dugi Otok** (52km/32 miles in length), is home to **Telašćica Bay** which can become packed with yachts, tour boats and even small cruise ships during summer. Telašćica is worthy of all the attention – a wide sweep of bay once prized by the Venetians as a safe anchorage. It is possible to walk around one side of the lake (**Lake Mir**, that breaks away from Telašćica Bay) and follow the path that eventually leads back out towards the sea on the other side. For those wanting to spend more time exploring the archipelago the town of **Sali**, with its sprinkling of hotels and pensions, is on hand.

Above: *St Donat's Church in Zadar's old Roman Forum.*

Kornati National Park ★★★

Further south towards the city of Šibenik is another necklace of islands, the famous **Kornati Islands**, which were memorably eulogized by George Bernard Shaw: 'On the last day of the Creation God desired to crown his work, and thus created the Kornati Islands out of tears, stars and breath.' The Kornati National Park is indeed a paradise of brilliant white islands, blue seas

> **SAILING**
>
> With 1185 islands and often idyllic sea conditions, particularly in the more sheltered areas of the Adriatic, it is hardly surprising that Croatia has emerged as a magnet for sailors in recent years. The most popular itineraries include trips around the Kornati islands, southern Dalmatia and the Zadar archipelago. Bareback charters, fully crewed hire and one-way sails are all available. Mooring space in the main tourist centres is at a premium in summer.

KORNATI ISLAND COTTAGES

Most people visit the Kornati Islands on a day trip from Šibenik or Zadar, while others moor their yachts offshore. Those who really want to experience the tranquil and desolate beauty of the archipelago can stay in one of 300 basic stone cottages on the islands. Cottages can be rented through travel agents based in Murter like **Coronata** (www.coronata.hr), **Kornat Turist** (www.kornatturist.hr), **Murter-Kornati** (www.murter-kornati.com) and **Žut Tours** (www.zuttours.hr).

and seemingly endless azure skies. In recent years this breathtaking archipelago has become popular with day-trippers and yachtsmen. Fortunately, among the 89 islands there are still many places to get away from it all and appreciate why Shaw was so besotted.

There are few more sublime experiences than spending a day sailing and swimming around the Kornati Islands before mooring in a tiny stone village and savouring a dinner of fresh seafood and fine Croatian wine, accompanied by home-made olive oil and freshly baked bread. For those not lucky enough to be on a yacht, day trips run from Zadar and Šibenik throughout the season. The national park was declared in 1980, though man had always struggled to manage much development here due to the lack of fresh water and the unfertile and thin soil base, with most of the islands already uninhabited by the time the national park was opened.

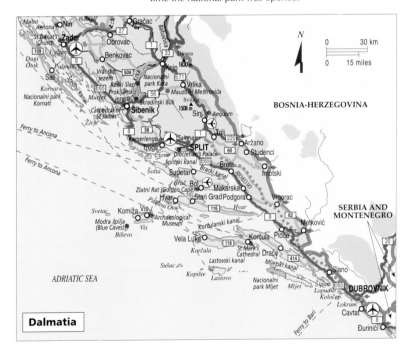

Dalmatia

Šibenik **

The northern Dalmatian coastal city of Šibenik
had its industries stripped away by Croatia's war
of independence and has a slightly forlorn ambience these days, but its spectacular cathedral
alone justifies the visit and its old quarter, which
largely escaped a Venetian-era makeover, is well
worth exploring. Šibenik is one of the country's
most 'Croatian' cities, playing a key role during
the first independent Croatia a millennium ago.
The best way of appreciating the different architectural styles is to meander up through the tight
cobweb of old-town streets as you ascend towards
Šibenik Castle. There is not much to do up here apart
from admire the views out towards the Adriatic, accessible through a narrow channel from the city, and peer
down into the warren-like old quarter below.

Above: *The Cathedral of
St James dominates the
Šibenik skyline.*

Cathedral of St James **

Šibenik's sublime Gothic and Renaissance creation,
crafted in the 15th and 16th centuries, was the work of
Dalmatian architects, such as Juraj Dalmatinac, and
Venetian master craftsmen. Dalmatinac never lived to
see his grand work completed, but a bronze statue,
sculpted by Ivan Meštrović, stands just outside to com-
memorate his work. Most of the (largely superficial)
damage from Serb shelling has now been repaired and
the cathedral is open to the public.

Features to look out for on the exterior include the
Gothic doorway, crowded with saints around its main
arch, and another portal that sports a suitably guilty
depiction of Adam, Eve and two rather Venetian-
looking lions. Perhaps the most remarkable part of
the cathedral's exterior are is **74 busts** that stare
down over the city. Local urban myth has it that these
were caricatures of various locals deemed too tight to
help foot the bill for the cathedral's construction.
Inside, key features of this triple-aisle cathedral are the
Baptistry, with its reliefs designed by Juraj Dalmatinac,
and **Tomb of St James**.

WATER SPORTS

The calm turquoise waters
of the Adriatic are becoming
increasingly popular with
water-sports enthusiasts, who
travel to Croatia to sea kayak,
windsurf, sail, water ski,
scuba dive and even take
part in swimming safaris. In
recent years the popularity
of white-water rafting on
Croatia's stunning rivers
including the Krka, which
flows through the Krka
National Park, has been
growing. Specialist operators
include: **Huck Finn**
(www.huck-finn.hr) and
VMD Travel (www.vmd.hr).
Activities can also be
arranged through the local
travel agents.

SAILING CELEBRETIES

Strolling along the waterfronts of Dalmatia's premier destinations – Trogir, Hvar, Korčula and Dubrovnik – during the summer months it can sometimes feel like you have stepped into the glamorous world of St Tropez, with luxurious yachts and plush motorboats moored for all to see. Celebrity owners reputed to have fallen for the irresistible charm of the Croatian Adriatic include Bill Gates, Bernie Eccelestone and Benetton.

Krka National Park **

A worthwhile excursion from the coast and a popular day trip from Zadar, Šibenik, and even Trogir or Split is to the spectacular waterfalls of Krka National Park. The Krka River, on its route between the mountains around Knin and its meeting with the sea near Šibenik, plunges over a series of waterfalls. Many locals insist these waterfalls are more impressive than the Plitvice Lakes, and they are certainly dramatic, particularly after heavy rain. Visiting the park is an especially enjoyable experience in summer as there is the opportunity to get into the river at **Skradinski Buk**, the only place where swimming is permitted. It is a short walk or boat ride here from **Skradin**, the tiny town that funnels visitors into the park. It is worth breaking away from the all too appealing waters and working your way up to **Visovac**, a small island with its own **Franciscan Monastery**, which guards a 15th-century edition of Aesop's Fables. Yet further on (there are national park boats on hand to ferry you along) are another stunning set of waterfalls, **Roški Slap**, and also an old Croatian fortress. All in all Krka makes for a perfect day trip.

CENTRAL DALMATIA
Trogir ***

Trogir is up there with Dubrovnik and Korčula when it comes to the accolade of being the Adriatic's most stunning coastal settlement, and UNESCO has recognized this status by placing the whole Old Town on its

Below: *Kamerlengo Fortress in Trogir's World Heritage listed Old Town.*

World Heritage List. Trogir is a compact town built on its own island, which is connected by bridges both to the mainland and to the larger island of Čiovo.

The town has been inhabited for over 4000 years, with traces of the different peoples who have lived in Trogir dotted around, inspiring today's 3000 inhabitants to dub their home the 'Town Museum'. If you are flying into Split's airport, look out for a unique aerial view of the city as you approach. A climb up the **Kamerlengo Fortress**, built by the Venetians in the 15th century to stave off the threat of Ottoman attack, also gives visitors an idea of Trogir's layout. From the fortress, stroll along the waterfront **Riva**, which bustles throughout the summer with seafood restaurants, pavement cafés, tour boats and the yachts of the rich and famous.

Above: *Trogir's waterfront Riva is very lively in summer.*

From the Riva little lanes lead enticingly into the web of medieval streets. Go through the 16th-century Town Gate and you ease down Gradska, which leads out into the open space of **Trg Ivana Pavla II**. In season a number of pavement cafés litter the square. In the southern corner is the 15th-century **Venetian loggia**. The loggia was subject of much controversy in the 20th century when locals tore off the Venetian lion emblem. Italian fascist dictator Mussolini vowed severe vengeance would be wrought, a threat that materialized with the outbreak of World War II and the Italian occupation of Croatia.

Trogir Cathedral ★★★

Trg Ivana Pavla II's real highlight is Trogir's voluminous **cathedral**. The **West Portal** (currently undergoing a major renovation) is a 13th-century masterpiece by Radovan. At the top are scenes from the life of Christ as well as images depicting local Dalmatian life, while the lower part would not win any politically correct prizes as the 'fallen' Adam and Eve are still above the Jews and Ottomans who appear to hold up the whole door.

Inside, the most arresting feature is **St John's Chapel**, the creation of Dalmatian architect Nikola Firentinac. The chapel is festooned with 160 sculpted heads of angels, cherubs and saints all culminating around God.

Riva *

On balmy summer evenings the Riva, with its wide expanse of stone benches and palm trees, is the place to be, as it explodes into life with jam-packed restaurants and cafés. The company reps trying to coax tourists into booking a boat trip the following day and the local youths that zip around on their mopeds infuse their own energy into the Riva.

SPLIT

A 30-minute drive south of Trogir, past the ruins of the Roman town of **Salona** and the crumbling mini-castles of **Kaštela** (both worth visiting in their own right), is Croatia's second largest city, Split. Many people only plan on transiting Split on one of the many ferries, but there is much to love about this buzzing, intoxicating Mediterranean port city and a longer stay is well rewarded.

Below: *Diocletian's Palace, still at the heart of modern-day Split.*

Diocletian's Palace ***

The epicentre of Split life is inside Diocletian's Palace, built between AD295 and 305 by the Roman Emperor Diocletian as his retirement home. Now recognized on **UNESCO's World Heritage List**, the palace complex is both a stunning Roman remnant and a testimony to the resourcefulness of the local people who have moulded it to their needs over the centuries. This is no museum piece, but a living and breathing, and yes, unfortunately often crumbling, urban oasis awash with apartments, cafés, bars and restaurants.

The best way into the complex is from the waterfront Riva through the **Bronze Gate**, which leads through an underground corridor (these days overflowing with souvenir stands) and spills out into the **Peristyle**, the palace's main attraction. The sunken Peristyle is surrounded by columns and is home to the Cathedral of St Domnius. This used to be the **Tomb of Emperor Diocletian** and the building's later ecclesiastical role is somewhat ironic given that Diocletian was a man said to have had a penchant for throwing Christians to the lions. The octagonal interior features what is claimed to be a portrait of Diocletian with his wife Prisca, and two altars –

Above: *Small boats bobbing along Split's waterfront.*

one by the Venetian sculptor Giovan Maria Morlaiter, and the other by Croatian Matija Pončun. Across from the cathedral is the **baptistry**, like much of the palace currently in the midst of a major renovation.

North of the Peristyle the old Roman thoroughfare leads up past **St Martin's Chapel** (the Christians built a chapel to safeguard each of the four main entrances) and the **Golden Gate**. Just outside the gate a small park is dominated by Ivan Meštrović's hulking statue of **Grgur Ninski** (*Grgur of Nin*).

Meštrović Gallery **

Grgur Ninski may be Meštrović's landmark work, but just around the bay west of the centre in the Marjan district is the Meštrović Gallery, which houses the largest collection of his work. He had intended this grand creation by the waterfront to be his home before he emigrated, like many Croats, to the USA. These days, now that Croatia is an independent country again, many exiles are coming back and rediscovering their roots.

Eating, Drinking and Nightlife **

Diocletian's former palace has its share of places to eat and drink (delve into the little explored upper level for the best bars) the most popular place to be on a sunny day or balmy evening is along the **Riva**. A clutch of cafés recline behind two waves of palm trees, making

IVAN MEŠTROVIĆ

Born in the Slavonian town of Vrpolje, Ivan Meštrović (1883–1962) spent his childhood in the Dalmatian town of Otavice before studying sculpture in Zagreb. Meštrović also honed his skills at the Academy of Fine Arts in Vienna and Paris before moving to Split. Today many of Meštrović's most famous works are on display in the Dalmatian capital's Meštrović Gallery, with one of his most famous carvings, the towering *Grgur of Nin*, guarding the northern gate of Diocletian's Palace.

Above: *Swimming off the Dalmatia coast in the clean waters of the Adriatic.*

for a relaxed scene, with the Jadrolinja ferries skipping between the Dalmatian islands and the mainland adding to the backdrop. After midnight the main action moves around to Split's most popular beach, **Bačvice**, where a modern entertainment complex awaits with lively restaurants, bars and discos.

CENTRAL DALMATIAN ISLANDS

As Croatia's main ferry hub Split is a great base for exploring the central Dalmatian islands, which can be done as a series of day trips for those short on time.

Brač **

The closest island is Brač, popular with those who commute to the city for work and increasingly with second homeowners from around Europe. Brač is world famous in the sense that its high-quality stone and marble has been used in a string of landmark buildings such as the **Hungarian Parliament** in Budapest and the **White House** in Washington DC. Unfortunately its dry stony terrain has made farming difficult over the centuries and much of the land, where it is not scarred by quarrying, is marked with man's attempts at cultivation.

The main ferry port is at the pleasant enough town of **Supetar**, but the drawcard is **Bol**, which attracts flights from Zagreb in summer thanks to its proximity to what many Croats regard as Croatia's finest beach. **Zlatni Rat** (Golden Cape) is certainly no travel secret and in summer the crowds are off-putting, but it is a divine spot. The shingle cape loops out into the crystal clear Adriatic waters in a striking teardrop shape, which changes with the tides and winds, with water lapping at both flanks. When the summer sun gets too much, a swathe of pine trees offers shade as well as scenting the air with a fresh aroma. Zlatni Rat often enjoys cooling breezes anyway, which makes it something of a Mecca

---

BRAČ STONE

Before tourism became the mainstay of the economy on the island of Brač, the third largest in Croatia, the islanders were largely dependent on money raised from the export of Brač stone and white marble. Famous throughout the world, Brač marble was used in the construction of Diocletian's Palace in Split, the White House in Washington DC, and the Reichstag in Berlin.

for windsurfers. Bol itself is a pleasant resort town, with hotels hidden behind a leafy promenade stretching between the town and Zlatni Rat.

Vidova Gora **

Walkers or any reasonably fit adult can embark on one of Dalmatia's greatest walks from Bol, following a path that reaches up 780m to the summit of **Vidova Gora**, the highest point amongst Croatia's 1185 islands. The summit offers sweeping views over Split, the Biokovo mountain range and out across the smattering of Dalmatian islands. It is possible to drive up to the summit and there is also a small restaurant that only opens in summer.

Hvar **

The island of Hvar, known locally as the 'long island', is aptly nicknamed as it sweeps along the Adriatic in a sinewy string south of Brač. Many locals claim that Hvar enjoys the sunniest climate in Croatia and it is said that at one time Hvar hoteliers put their money where their mouths were and offered refunds when the sun was not shining over this glamorous island. Whether it is the seemingly endless sunshine or the aroma of wild lavender which permeates the air, Hvar has a unique appeal that makes it one of Croatia's most popular island retreats.

Hvar Town ***

Ferries arrive in **Stari Grad** but most visitors make a bee-line for **Hvar Town** on the other side of the island. This is an idyllic Adriatic town, where impressive Venetian-era houses proudly line the broad waterfront and bay, helping usher in new arrivals who generally head straight towards the pavement cafés of the piazza. In August, Hvar Town can be frenetic, as the whole of Italy seems to descend and there is not a spare bed in town.

> **HVAR LAVENDER**
>
> *Lavandula Croatica* (Croatian Lavender) is one of Hvar's biggest sources of revenue. Year-round sunshine produces a climate perfect for growing lavender, which has blossomed on the island's rocky hillsides since at least the 1930s. The scale of production ranges from small family businesses to larger corporate concerns, but for most visitors the only visible signs of the industry are the many lotions and oils on sale at stalls in Hvar Town.

Below: *Hvar Town's popular waterfront.*

The Piazza **

The Piazza is the informal name of **Trg Sveti Stjepana**, but one that almost all locals use. It starts by the **Štandarac Column**, where long ago official proclamations were announced to the largely illiterate population of Hvar Town. This end of the square, more of a long rectangle in reality, is also home to the **Venetian Arsenal**, where the Divine Republic's ships were once mended before being launched into another round of trade or battle. The upper level was later remoulded into one of Croatia's first public theatres and it still stands today. At the opposite end of the square is **St Stephen's Cathedral**, erected on the site of a Benedictine Monastery that was obliterated by the Ottoman Turks. Look out for the delicate 13th-century *Madonna and Child* on the altar inside the cathedral.

Swimming Around Hvar Town **

Just a short walk east of the town hotels and restaurants huddle around stretches of beach that get very crowded in summer. A better option if you are looking for a swim is to take a boat out to the rather dubious sounding **Pakleni Otoci**, which translates as the 'Islands of Hell'. Fortunately there is nothing satanic about them, though more conservatively minded bathers may want to avoid **Jerolim** where dispensing with all clothing is the norm and head for the more mainstream beaches on **Sveti** and **Marinkovac**. Water taxis charging fixed prices run between Hvar Town and all three beaches throughout the summer season.

Below: *Relaxing in a café in Vis Town.*

Vis **

Vis, one of the most remote of the Croatian islands, has a magical and unspoilt quality to it, perhaps partly because it spent decades during Tito's reign as an off-limits naval base, only reopening to the public in 1989. Vis has always been a prized property given its strategic locale, with views out to the Dalmatian coast on one flank and the

Italian littoral on the other. The British used Vis as a base in World War II when they plotted the downfall of the Germans and mounted commando raids alongside Tito and his Partisans. From the sea the island exhibits the rugged beauty of a Scottish Hebridean isle and there seems to be no prospect of a landing spot, until the ferry sweeps around into the wide bay of Vis Town.

Vis Town **

Amongst the scattering of buildings that line the waterfront there are a couple of worthwhile places to visit, including the **Franciscan Monastery**, whose most interesting feature is its graveyard. Wander among the headstones and you will find one commemorating the life of Toma Brananović, the work of Dalmatian sculptor Ivan Rendić. Another striking memorial pays homage to the Austrian sailors killed in a naval engagement off Vis in 1866. A fifteen-minute walk back past the ferry landing brings you to the **Church of Our Lady of the Cave**. The triple-nave interior is quite remarkable; however, the very visible collection boxes give some indication of the urgent need for renovation. The most striking piece of art is the *Madonna with the Saints* by Girolamo da Santacroce.

Archaeological Museum *

Around the corner from the church is the Archaeological Museum, easily visible thanks to the British cannons that lie outside. Perhaps the most poignant feature is not really on display at all – as you enter look out for a rather forlorn statue of **Tito**, once the hero of Yugoslavia, lying dumped against a wall. Inside the museum there is a decent amount to see, with a large collection of amphorae recovered from a Greek ship that may have sunk off Vis as long ago as the 4th century BC. These are just part of the legacy on show that shed light on the important role the Greeks played in the history of Vis.

Above: *Vis Town's Archaeological Museum with its collection of amphorae.*

SCUBA DIVING

There has been a recent explosion in Croatia's popularity as a scuba diving destination, with divers flocking here to explore beneath the surface of the country's calm Adriatic waters. Trial dives, night dives and certified courses are offered by the majority of operators, with some of the best dives taking in the Blue Grotto at Biševo and ships wrecked off the island of Vis. Regulations are available from **Hrvatski Ronilački Savez** (the Croatian Diving Association) at www.diving-hrs.hr

Above: *St Michael's Church, overlooking the town of Komiža.*

Kut **

The most attractive corner of Vis Town is further around the bay in Kut. This was where wealthy Venetian merchants once chose to build their homes, and their fine houses and palazzi recline in this elegant part of town. These days old women hang out their washing from Venetian-era balconies, and a number of excellent restaurants have taken up residence. Choose from **Pojoda** (Don C. Marasovića 8), **Vatrica** (Obala Kralja KreĐmira IV 13) and **Kaliopa** (Vladmira Nazora 32) and you won't be disappointed, especially if you love seafood. Kaliopa is extra special thanks to its setting, lying amidst a sculpture-strewn garden set back from the waterfront. Kut is also worth visiting thanks to the small wine producers who offer their wares from their own homes – look out for the 'Domaće Vino Pradjem' signs.

Komiža *

Travel over the steep hills of Vis, home to the cave where Tito once sought refuge from the Germans, and you come down to the unassuming town of Komiža. Here the comings and goings of the fishing fleet are the only brief flurries of activity to break the calm. In the midst of the centre is the **Fishing Museum**, housed in a small old castle, worth popping into. Also worth a look when you are descending into Komiža is the **Church of St Michael** and the old monastery beside it. A church has stood here among the vine-covered slopes guarding over the Adriatic since the 12th century, with today's incarnation dating mainly from the 17th century.

Biševo's Blue Cave ***

Most visitors come to Komiža for one thing – to use it as a springboard to get to the neighbouring islet of Biševo's famed Blue Cave, which Croatians like to compare with Capri's Blue Grotto. Inside this small cave the Adriatic water combines with the sunlight to create a stunning blue light. The light show only really works during good weather and you would not want to be out here in a small boat when the sea is choppy anyway. The gaggle of local operators only run trips out in decent weather and this is the way that most people choose to visit the Blue Cave. Alternatively operators in Vis Town can organize scuba diving trips to the cave for a truly unique and memorable perspective on this remarkable natural phenomenon.

The Makarska Riviera *

While the Makarska Riviera is massively popular with Bosnians and citizens of the former Soviet Union, it does not appeal to everyone. There are numerous hotels along the coast south of Split towards the Bosnian border and that is part of the problem, as so much development has led to much of the scenic splendour being spoiled. One saving grace is the rugged sweep of the Biokovo mountain range that rises up behind the string of resorts. During the off-peak seasons when you can snare yourself a good patch of beach the Makarska Riviera can be pleasant enough, but you are usually more likely to have to fight for space amid the crowds in the resorts of **Brela**, **Baška Voda**, **Tučepi**, **Podgora**, **Gradac** and **Makarska** itself.

SOUTHERN DALMATIA
Korčula ***

This island claims to have been the birth-place of legendary explorer **Marco Polo** and the locals also assert that he came back to spend his last days here after decades of wandering the globe. It is easy to see why, as this is one of the prettiest of all the Adriatic islands, with lush vine-covered slopes and the exceptional beauty of **Korčula Town**. The willowy island, much of which is lavishly cloaked in pine trees and green scrub, stretches for 47km (29 miles) from east to west and is never more than 7km (4.5 miles) in width. Its indented coastline wraps around numerous bays, coves and inlets.

> **TRAIN TRIP TO SARAJEVO**
>
> One of the most appealing railway journeys in central Europe is the line that runs between the Croatian port of Ploče and Sarajevo, cutting through Bosnia-Herzegovina's rugged mountains and travelling via Mostar en route. For those wanting to visit the Bosnian capital an alternative route also exists with the recent recommencement of the direct service going from Zagreb to Sarajevo.

Below: *The stunning Makarska Riviera and its main resort of Makarska.*

MOREŠKA DANCE

During the peak tourist season regular performances of the Moreška Folk Dance see a skilful sword dance liven up the tranquil pace of life in Korčula's Old Town. Historically, the Moreška symbolizes the triumph of Christianity over Islam, but the story played out today is more simplistic and shows the white (Christian) king and the black (Turkish) king fighting for the affections of a fair maiden. Supporters of each king are drawn into the battle, resulting in a series of seven impressive dances.

Korčula was first settled by the Greeks who dubbed it 'Black Corfu', given its mass of woodland, but it was the Venetians who had the greatest impact on Korčula, arriving in the 10th century and lingering for another 800 years, leaving an impressive architectural legacy. By the 20th century Korčula had lost its strategic importance and settled into a comfortable middle age, but today the island is experiencing something of a renaissance as one of Croatia's rising tourist stars.

Korčula Town ***

This dizzyingly attractive collection of old stone houses, crumbling churches and cobbled streets spreads out across its own peninsula and is the island's main drawcard. Exploring Korčula Town is easy with a thoroughfare running right through the heart of the old core and a waterside boulevard circling the peninsula.

St Mark's Cathedral *

Korčula Town's most dramatic building is St Mark's Cathedral. This triple-naved basilica's interior impresses with a cocktail of architectural styles where Gothic and Renaissance take centre stage. One of the most unusual aspects of the cathedral's façade is the single figure of a woman who is surrounded by a gaggle of monsters, but no one really seems to know exactly who she is, though some suggest that she was the wife of Emperor Diocletian. The cathedral is also home to an *Annunciation* by celebrated Italian artist Tintoretto, who spent time in Korčula as a student. The altarpiece on the wall of the apse carries depictions of the saints Bartholomew, Jerome and Mark, the patron saints of Korčula, who were said to have helped stave off the attentions of the Ottomans when they besieged the town on the way north to the **Battle of Lepanto** in the 16th century. Art lovers

Below: *Korčula Town's old quarter enjoys its own promontory.*

should also head next door to the **Bishop's Treasury**, which crams a surprising amount of works by an eclectic array of artists into its small confines. The building itself was restored in the 17th century with the addition of a hanging garden.

Marco Polo House *

Given the level of local pride it is nigh impossible to resist a visit to the Marco Polo House, where the explorer is said to have been born in 1254. Most scholars agree that Polo spent at least some time in Korčula, so the legend may well be true. There is actually little to see inside the house, but the walk to the top floor is well worth it for the sweeping vista of terracotta-tiled roofs, clear blue sea and pine-clad hills. The great explorer is remembered in the annual **Marco Polo Festival**, which is held in May.

Above: *Locals celebrating the Marco Polo Festival in Korčula Town.*

Dubrovnik ***

Dubrovnik, for most visitors to Croatia, is quite simply the most stunning city in the country, a paradise up there with anywhere else they have visited around the world. Lord Byron shared this opinion; the poet was so smitten with the one-time city-state that he eulogized it as the 'Pearl of the Adriatic'. Backed by steep limestone crags to the rear and fronted by the sublimely blue waters of the Adriatic, this perfectly preserved gem is encompassed within sturdy medieval walls, which house a cocktail of Baroque churches and palaces.

Dubrovnik (once known as Ragusa) survived for centuries as an independent republic whose motto was *Libertas* (freedom), standing up against the powerful Venetians to the north as well as the Ottomans to the south with the sort of skilful negotiation and double-dealing that Machiavelli would have been proud of. Dubrovnik's citizens boast that their thick city walls have never been breached, though they, and the resolve of the inhabitants, were tested in the winter of

MARCO POLO

The residents of Korčula, like the citizens of Genoa and Venice, swear that Marco Polo was born on their island, and point doubting visitors in the direction of the Marco Polo House. It is possible that Marco Polo was, as is claimed, born on Korčula as evidence suggests that he did at least visit the island. The Marco Polo Festival, held every May, celebrates the homecoming of the great explorer who is said to have chosen to return to his treasured birthplace after his wanderings.

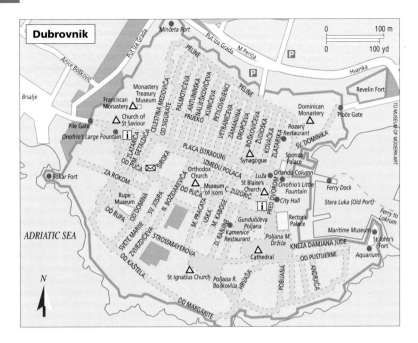

1991–92 when Serb and Montenegrin paramilitaries, backed up the might of the Yugoslav National Army, navy and air force, laid siege to a city that had no real strategic value or Serb claim to ownership. This brutal act of cultural vandalism helped bring Europe round to the Croatian cause.

Today the only legacies of the siege are the swathe of new roof tiles – easily spotted by their new shade (the original quarry had long since closed down) – and the large board as you enter the Old Town, which marks where the shells hit. Today the tourist crowds are back in Dubrovnik as it reclaims its title as the 'Pearl of the Adriatic.'

City Walls ***

Anyone able to should not miss the opportunity to walk around the wide curl of the city walls. The rugged stone walls loop up around the city skirting the harsh limestone crags to the north and then pass the old port before scooping back around the coast where the Adriatic laps against its voluminous bastions. You can walk around in an hour, but it is better to take one of the audio tours – pick up a headset at the ticket counters on your way up to the walls – and spend your time learning about Dubrovnik's history.

The Stradun **

Dubrovnik's main thoroughfare (also locally known as the Placa) spreads right through the pedestrianized heart of the Old Town. Formed when the channel that separated Ragusa from the mainland was filled in during the 12th century, today the thoroughfare bustles with tourists in summer and boasts a wealth of cafés, bars, shops and restaurants. Despite the crowds, the Stradun still retains its charm thanks to strict controls on development that ensure that the wooden shutters on windows as well as lampposts are all the same colour.

Franciscan Monastery **

This monastery complex lies just off the Stradun – make sure to come early if a cruise ship is in town to avoid the crowds. The single-nave **Church of St Francis** is in itself fairly unspectacular, but the **Monastery Treasury Museum** is worth venturing into with a range of exhibits taken from the monastery. The complex also boasts attractive 14th-century cloisters, a still functioning pharmacy (said to be the oldest in the country) and a series of religious paintings.

Sponza Palace *

Look out for the 'We are forbidden to cheat and use false measures, and when I weigh goods, God weighs me,' motto which tells you all you need to know about one of the former roles of this grace-

Below: *Dubrovnik's unparalleled Old Town overlooks the Adriatic.*

DUBROVNIK SUMMER FESTIVAL

In July and August the world-famous Dubrovnik Summer Festival brings traditional, classical and contemporary productions to indoor and outdoor stages throughout the Old Town. The local name for the festival is *Libertas* (liberty), a name that originates from the days when Dubrovnik was an independent republic, and whose sentiment was poignantly felt in the early 1990s when the shells falling on the city didn't halt the festival.

ful palace on the Stradun. The 14th-century palace used to function as Ragusa's customs house and mint, but today it is home to the State Archives and is also a cultural venue during the **Dubrovnik Festival**.

St Blaise's Church **

This 18th-century Baroque church is dedicated to the city's patron saint and lies at the head of the Stradun at the point where it unfurls into Luža Square. Inside, St Blaise proudly cradles a model of his beloved city, revealing what Dubrovnik looked like before the devastating 17th-century earthquake. If you are in town on St Blaise Day (3 February) you will see the statue of the saint being trooped around the Old Town.

Rector's Palace **

Just a short stroll off the Stradun is the former home of the city's old rector. Unlike the case with many despots of the time, democratic Dubrovnik did not let him outgrow his boots and he had a limited term in office, during which he was largely banned from leaving the palace except on official business. Today the courtyard is a venue for traditional dancing and music in summer, and there is a dimly lit museum in the upper level whose displays explore the history and life in the time of the Ragusa Republic.

Below: *The grand Rector's Palace in Dubrovnik's Old Town.*

Cathedral *

Legend has it that the original cathedral was built by **Richard the Lionheart** of England as a thank you that his life had been spared in a violent storm off Dubrovnik. This Baroque incarnation comes complete with three aisles and a large cupola that dominates the city skyline. The **Treasury** is home to gold and silver artefacts as well as the skull, arm and leg of the St Balise himself, presented in lavish Byzantine style.

Relaxing in the Old Town ★★★
Spending time in Dubrovnik is a pleasure thanks to the numerous cafés, bars and restaurants, many of them blessed with outdoor terraces to take advantage of the idyllic Mediterranean climate. Prijeko is a whole street full of inexpensive restaurants, though quality can falter at the height of season. A better bet for an inexpensive meal is **Kamenice** in Gundulićeva poljana, which dishes up huge portions of seafood risotto and spaghetti. At the other end of the scale upmarket **Atlas Club Nautika** just outside the Old Town by the Pile Gate concentrates on fine dining with views back towards the old city walls. The Stradun is the place to see and be seen as the hub of café life, though come early to have any hope of snaring a prized outdoor seat during the Dubrovnik Festival. Other nightlife includes **cultural performances** in the Sponza and Rector's palaces, and there are a couple of discos outside the old town that are busy during the summer.

Above: *Dubrovnik and the neighbouring island of Lokrum.*

Southern Dalmatian Islands ★★
Dubrovnik makes a good base for exploring the Southern Dalmatian islands, all of them accessible on day trips. There is **Mljet**, a green and lush jewel, much of which is protected as a national park. You can rent bikes here and circle around the network of paths and lakes, or just go for a stroll, punctuated perhaps by a swim in one of the national park's lakes. The smaller **Elaphiti Islands** (**Koločep**, **Lopud and Čipan**) are also becoming increasingly popular. For those short on time there is always **Lokrum**, the thickly forested little islet that lies just offshore and is clearly visible from Dubrovnik. Regular boats run out in season from Dubrovnik's old port, with the chance to explore the coves and beaches of this uninhabited island.

ADVANCE RESERVATIONS

Hotel accommodation tends to get booked up quickly during the summer months. This is especially true in Dubrovnik during the city's Summer Festival (Jul–Aug), making it a good idea to book ahead. When making an advance reservation it is best to choose somewhere that is registered with the Croatian National Tourist Board unless you have a reliable personal recommendation. Hotels with their own websites let you see what you are paying for.

Dalmatia at a Glance

BEST TIMES TO VISIT

Tourist facilities in Dalmatia's cities are open year-round. **Apr–Jun** are best – the weather is good, but the crowds have not yet descended. Tourism practically shuts down on the islands between Nov and Mar.

GETTING THERE

By Air: International flights serve Split, Dubrovnik and Zadar airports.
By Road: A comprehensive bus service connects towns and cities in Dalmatia to the rest of Croatia. International services run to Dubrovnik, Split, Šibenik and Zadar.
By Rail: The railway between Zagreb and Split is being up-graded to provide a faster link.
By Boat: Split is Jadrolinija's main ferry port, with boats to and from Dalmatia's islands, as well as Rijeka and, in the summer, Zadar. Ferries from Italy and Greece also dock in Split and Dubrovnik.

GETTING AROUND

Limited bus services operate on the islands of Brač, Hvar and Korčula, but you will need a car to explore them fully. Split, Zadar, Šibenik and Dubrovnik have bus services.

WHERE TO STAY

Zadar
MID-RANGE
Hotel Kolovare, Boże Peričića 14, tel: 023 203 200, fax: 023 203 300, www.tel.hr/hotel-kolovare-zadar Business-style hotel with outdoor pool just 10 minutes from the Old Town.

Šibenik
MID-RANGE
Hotel Jadran, tel: 022 212 644, fax: 022 212 480. Šibenik's only central hotel.

Trogir
MID-RANGE
Hotel Fontana, Obrov 1, tel: 021 885 744, fax: 021 885 755, www.tel.hr/fontana-commerce Modern and good sized rooms.

Split
LUXURY
Hotel Park, Hatzeov Perivoj 3, tel: 021 406 400, fax: 021 406 401, www.hotelpark-split.hr Excellent hotel just back from Bačvice beach.
MID-RANGE
Hotel Split, Put Trstenika 19, tel: 021 303 011, www.hotel split.hr Modern rooms with balconies and sea views, 3km (2 miles) from the Old Town.

Brač
MID-RANGE
Hotel Ivan, David 11a, tel: 021 640 888, fax: 021 640 846, www.hotel-ivan.com Small hotel in an old stone house; outdoor pool.

Hvar Town
MID-RANGE
Hotel Slavija, tel: 021 741 820, fax: 021 741 147, www.suncanihvar.hr Harbourfront hotel with basic rooms.

Vis Town
BUDGET
Hotel Restaurant Paula, Petra Hektorovića 2, tel: 021 711 362, fax: 021 711 362, www.hinet.hr/paula-hotel Charming family-run hotel in the heart of the Old Town.

Korčula
LUXURY
Hotel Korčula, Obala Vinka Paletina, tel: 020 711 078, fax: 020 711 746. A historic building, waterfront location; a popular choice.

Makarska
MID-RANGE
Biokovo, Kralja Tomislava bb, tel: 021 615 224, fax: 021 615 081, www.hotelbiokovo.hr Popular waterfront hotel.

Dubrovnik
LUXURY
The Excelsior Hotel, Frana Suplia 12, tel: 020 414 222, fax: 020 414 214, www.hotel-excelsior.hr Five-star hotel offering stun-ning vistas of the Old Town.
MID-RANGE
Bellevue, Pera Čingrije 7, tel: 020 413 306, fax: 020 414 058, www.hotel-bellevue.hr Balconied rooms overlooking bay, 15 mins from old core.
BUDGET
Dubrovnik Youth Hostel, Vinka Sagrestana 3, tel: 020 423 241, fax: 020 412 592. Within walking distance of Dubrovnik's historic centre.

WHERE TO EAT

Šibenik
Gradska Vijećnica, Trg Republike Hrvatske 3, tel: 022 213 605. Superb views of Šibenik's cathedral.

Zadar
Foša, Foša 2, tel: 023 314

Dalmatia at a Glance

421, fax: 023 212 515. Fresh
seafood cooked to perfection.
Dubrovnik
Atlas Club Nauticka, Brsalje
3, tel: 020 442 526, fax: 020
222 525. Fine dining just out-
side the Pile gate.
Kamenica, Gundulićeva pol-
jana 8. Great value no-frills
fish restaurant.
Hvar
Macondo, Avelinija, tel: 021
741 851. Classy, popular fish
restaurant. Book ahead.
Makarska
Biokovo (see Where to Stay).
Choose from the fine dining
restaurant or informal pizzeria.
Mali Ston
Vila Koruna (see Where to
Stay). Fish so fresh you choose
it from a tank. A glass conser-
vatory with great views.
Split
Stellon, Bačvice. Stylish
Italian; affordable pizza and
pasta, more innovative mains.
Noštromo, Kraj svete Marije
8. Up-market fish restaurant
in the heart of the Old Town.
Brač
Taverna Riva, Frane Radića 5,
Bol, tel: 021 635 236, www.
riva-bol.com Serving good
Croatian food with pleasant
views across to Hvar.
Trogir
Restoran Fontana (see Where
to Stay). Classy restaurant
serving Adriatic fish staples.
Vis
Villa Kaliopa, V. Nazora 32,
tel: 021 711 755. Enjoy a
decadent feast in a candlelit
sculpture garden.

SHOPPING

Split's Old Town is brimming
with shops selling everything
from Italian shoes to designer
gear with big name brands
like Benetton and Hugo Boss.

TOURS AND EXCURSIONS

VMD Travel Agency organize
a walk to the secluded
Gagolitic Monastery on Brač.
Trips to the Kornati Islands
from Murter, Krka National
Park from Šibenik and the
Elaphite Islands from
Dubrovnik are also popular.

USEFUL CONTACTS

VWM Travel Agency, 3
Cvjetno naselje 20, Zagreb,
tel: 01 606 5840, fax: 01 606
5841, www.vmd.hr
Kornati National Park, Butina
2, Murter, tel: 022 434 662,
fax: 022 435 058,
www.tel.hr/np-kornati
Mljet National Park,
Pristaniste 2, Govedari, tel:
020 744 041, fax: 020 744
043, www.np-mljet.hr
Krka National Park, Trg Ivana
Pavla II 5, Šibenik, tel: 022
217 720, fax: 022 336 836,
www.npkrka.hr
Bol (Brač) Tourist Informa-

tion, Porat Bolskih Pomoraca
bb, tel; 021 635 638, fax: 021
635 972, www.bol.hr
Dubrovnik Tourist Informa-
tion, Cvijete Zuzorić 1/ll, tel:
020 323 887, fax: 020 323
725, http://dubrovnik.laus.hr
Hvar Tourist Information, Trg
Svetog Stjepana 21, tel: 021
741 059, fax: 021 741 059,
www.hvar.hr
Makarska Tourist Informa-
tion, Obala kralja Tomislava
16, tel: 021 612 002, fax: 021
612 002, www.dalmacija.net/
makarska.htm
Šibenik Tourist Information,
Fausta Vrančića 18, tel: 022
212 075, fax: 022 219 073,
www.summernet.hr/sibenik
Krka National Park, Trg Ivana
Pavla II 5, tel: 022 217 720,
fax: 022 336 836, www.
npkrka.hr
Split Tourist Information,
Peristil bb, tel: 021 342 606,
www.visitsplit.com
Trogir Tourist Information,
Obala Bana Berislavića 12,
tel: 021 881 412, www.
dalmacija.net/trogir.htm
Zadar Tourist Information,
Llije Smiljanića 5, tel: 023
212 412, fax: 023 211 781,
www.zadar.hr

SPLIT	J	F	M	A	M	J	J	A	S	O	N	D
AVERAGE TEMP. °C	7.4	8.1	10.4	13.9	18.4	22.4	25.4	25.2	21.4	16.9	12.2	8.7
AVERAGE TEMP. °F	45	46	50	55	64	71	76	76	70	62	53	48
HOURS OF SUN DAILY	4.1	5.1	5.7	7.1	8.7	10	11.1	10.2	8.3	6.5	4.4	3.9
RAINFALL mm	82.7	68.1	75.3	65.5	56.3	50.8	28.3	50.2	60.6	78.7	108.4	99.6
RAINFALL in	3.26	2.68	2.96	2.58	2.27	2	1.11	1.98	2.39	3.09	4.23	3.92
DAYS OF RAINFALL	9	8	8	8	6	6	3	4	5	7	10	10

Travel Tips

Tourist Information

Croatian National Tourist Board, Iblerov trg 10/4, 10000 Zagreb, tel: 385 1 469 9333, fax: 385 1 455 7827, e-mail: info@htz.hr
website: www.croatia.hr

Main overseas offices:

UK: 2 Lanchesters, 162-164 Fulham Palace Road, London W6 9ER, tel: 44 20 8563 7979, fax: 22 40 8563 2616, e-mail: info@cnto.freeserve.co.uk, website: http://gb.croatia.hr

USA: 350 Fifth Avenue, Suite 4003, New York 10118, tel: 1 212 279 8672 or toll free 1 800 829 4416, fax: 1 212 279 8683, e-mail: cntony@earthlink.net
website: http://us.croatia.hr

Germany: Rumfordstrasse 7, München 80469, tel: 49 89 223 344, fax: 44 89 223 377, e-mail: kroatien-tourismus @t-online.de
website: http://de.croatia.hr

Italy: Via Dell'Oca 48, Roma 00186, tel: 39 06 3211 0396, fax: 39 06 3211 1462, e-mail: officeroma@enteturismo croato.it
website: http://it.croatia.hr

France: 48 avenue Victor Hugo, Paris 75116, tel: 33 1 4500 9955, fax: 33 1 4500 9956, e-mail: CROATIE.OT@wanadoo.fr website: http://fr.croatia.hr

Austria: Am Hof 13, Wien 1010, tel: 43 1 585 3884, fax: 43 1 585 3884 20, e-mail: office@kroatien.at
website: http://at.croatia.hr

Entry Requirements

You need a valid passport to enter Croatia and the majority of visitors, including those from North and South America, New Zealand, Australia and Europe, may stay for up to 90 days without any further documentation. Most Africans, including South Africans, need a visa to enter the country and should get advice from a Croatian embassy or consulate office.

Croatian embassies and consulates:

UK: 21 Conway Street, London W1T 6BN, tel: 44 20 7387 2022, fax: 44 20 7387 0936, e-mail: croemb.london @mvp.hr, website: http://uk.mfa.hr

USA: 2343 Massachusetts Ave, NW Washington DC 20008-2803, tel: 1 202 588 5899, fax: 1 202 558 8937, e-mail: public@croatiaemb.org website: www.croatiaemb.org

Germany: Ahornstraße 4, Berlin 10787, tel: 49 30 2191 5514, fax: 49 30 2362 8965, e-mail: vrh.berlin@mvp.hr

Italy: Via Luigi Bodio 74/76, Roma 00191, tel: 39 06 3630 7650, fax: 39 06 3630 3405, e-mail: croatian.embassy. roma@mvp.hr

France: 39 avenue Georges Mandel, Paris 75116, tel: 33 1 5370 0280, fax: 33 1 5370 0290, e-mail: redaction@ amb-croatie.fr website: www.amb-croatie.fr

Austria: Heuberggasse 10, Wien 1170, tel: 43 1 485 9524, fax: 43 1 480 2942, e-mail: croem.bec@mvp.hr

Customs

Croatian customs officials will allow you to enter Croatia with personal possessions up to the value of 300 HRK (see Money Matters), 200 cigarettes/ 250 g tobacco/50 cigars/100 cigarillos, 2 litres of liqueur, 2 litres of wine, 1 litre of spirits, 50g perfume and 250ml eau de toilette without having to pay customs duties.

Health Requirements

You do not need any inoculations to visit Croatia. Many European governments have a reciprocal health agreement with Croatia, including the British and Irish governments, which allow their citizens to receive free emergency medical attention.

Getting There

By Air: Croatia Airlines (www.croatiaairlines.hr) fly direct from locations across Europe to the international airports at Zagreb, Split, Zadar and Pula. The national carrier also operates domestic routes within Croatia.

By Road: Croatia shares land borders with Slovenia, Serbia and Montenegro, Hungary and Bosnia-Herzegovina, making it accessible by road from all over Europe. International buses connect Croatia to its neighbouring countries and other European cities.

By Rail: Direct international rail services from Austria, Bosnia-Herzegovina, Germany, Hungary, Italy, Switzerland, Slovenia and Serbia and Montenegro all run to Croatia.

By Boat: Ferries and catamarans to Croatia operate from Italy (Ancona, Venice, Trieste and Bari). There are public marinas where you can moor your yacht all along the Croatian coastline.

What to Pack

Sunglasses, a sunhat, sunscreen and lightweight clothing that lets your skin breathe are all essential summer items. In winter the picture is dramatically different with temperatures in the capital and the north of the country in general often plummeting below 0°C. Even on the coast it is cold at night, so those visiting at this time of year need to pack a warm coat. Casual clothing is acceptable almost everywhere, with smart casual the norm in more expensive restaurants. Photocopies of any important documents, such as your passport and travel insurance, are also a good idea.

Money Matters

Currency: Croatia's national currency is the Kuna (HRK), with 1 Kuna made up of 100 lipa. Prices are often also quoted in euros.

Currency Exchange: Cash can be exchanged at Croatian banks, hotels, travel agencies and exchange offices. Traveller's cheques can be changed in banks and some travel agencies. Euros, US dollars and British pounds are easy to change.

Debit and Credit Cards: Maestro, Mastercard, Visa, Cirrus cards, American Express and Diners Club International are commonly accepted. They can also be used in ATMs to withdraw money.

Money Transfers: A large number of post offices can arrange money transfers.

Tipping: A service charge is usually included in the bill; however, it is courteous to round bills up to the nearest 10 HRK.

DATES	
Days of the Week	
Ponedjeljak	– Monday
Utorak	– Tuesday
Srijeda	– Wednesday
Četvrtak	– Thursday
Petak	– Friday
Subota	– Saturday
Nedjelja	– Sunday
Months of the Year	
Siječanj	– January
Veljača	– February
Ožujak	– March
Travanj	– April
Svibanj	– May
Lipanj	– June
Srpanj	– July
Kolovoz	– August
Rujan	– September
Listopad	– October
Studeni	– November
Prosinac	– December

VAT: Value Added Tax is charged at 22% in Croatia. Non-Croatians can claim their VAT back on transactions over 500 HRK when they leave.

Accommodation

Croatia has a range of accommodation options from camp sites and private rooms or apartments, to graded hotels (1–5 star) and even restored lighthouses. A growing number of small family-run hotels are also springing up. Facilities and room rates vary greatly, but standards are generally high.

Eating Out

Croatian eateries are loosely classified as restaurants (*restoran/restauracija*), taverns (*konoba*) and inns (*gostilna*), with a descending degree of formality in each of those listed. In practice these distinctions are often blurred or not made at all. Snacks and cakes are also often served in cafés, and *slastičarnice* – a cross between a patisserie and an ice cream shop – are very popular with Croatians. The country's national cuisine is heavily influenced by neighbouring countries, with hearty meat staples dominating menus in the hinterland, and fresh Adriatic fish in abundance along the coast. Italian-style pizzerias have also popped up all over Croatia. An increasing number of international restaurants are opening up in Croatia, although there is little diversity compared to many other European cities outside of Zagreb. In the capital you can find everything from Indian to Japanese dishes.

Transport

Air: Croatia Airlines operate internal flights from Zagreb to Split, Dubrovnik, Pula, Rijeka, Zadar and, during peak season, Brač. There are also seasonal departures from Osijek to Dubrovnik and Split. It is generally cheaper to book internal flights inside Croatia.

Road: Croatia has a comprehensive network of paved roads, making it possible to drive virtually anywhere. Although new highways are under construction, single-lane roads, including most of the main coastal road, the Jadranksa Magistrala (or the Adriatic Highway), serve much of the country.

Buses: Catching the bus is a viable alternative to driving. Many operators run air-conditioned services all over the country. Fares are reasonable, with a six-hour journey between Zagreb and Split costing around 140 HRK.

Trains: Croatia's rail network is slow and limited, though recent improvements and investment in infrastructure are starting to make trains more attractive.

Trams: City trams operate in Zagreb and Osijek.

Taxis: Croatia's main towns and cities have a plentiful supply of taxis. Fares are reasonable with flag falls of 25–30HRK and then a charge of 6–7HRK a kilometre.

Ferry: Jadrolinija operate over 30 domestic ferry services between the mainland and Croatia's islands.

Business Hours

Office Hours: Mon–Fri 08:00–16:00.

Post Offices: Mon–Fri 07:00–19:00 and Sat 07:00–13:00.

Banks: Mon–Fri 07:00–19:00. In small towns and tourist resorts many banks and post offices close early, or operate a split shift.

Time Difference

GMT +1 hour

Communications

Post: HPT Hrvatska operate Croatia's postal service. Expect airmail post to take up to five days to reach other European countries and up to two weeks for Australia, New Zealand and North America. Other post

CONVERSION CHART

FROM	TO	MULTIPLY BY
Millimetres	Inches	0.0394
Metres	Yards	1.0936
Metres	Feet	3.281
Kilometres	Miles	0.6214
Square kilometres	Square miles	0.386
Hectares	Acres	2.471
Litres	Pints	1.760
Kilograms	Pounds	2.205
Tonnes	Tons	0.984
To convert Celsius to Fahrenheit: x 9 ÷ 5 + 32		

office services include fax, telephone card sale, credit card cash advances and currency exchange.

Telephone: You can make a direct local, national or international call from any public telephone in Croatia using a phone card. When placing a local call omit the two-digit area code (e.g. 01 for Zagreb); this needs to be dialled if the call is national. The country dialling code for Croatia is 385.

Fax: You can send and receive faxes in most of the more expensive hotels, as well as at some post offices.

Internet Cafés: These can be found in Croatia's larger towns and cities, as well as in tourist resorts. They are generally open seven days a week from 08:00–23:00. Charges range from 10–30 HRK per hour.

Electricity

220 volts, 50 AC. European two-pin round pronged plugs are used throughout Croatia.

Weights and Measures

Croatia uses a metric system with distances measured in kilometres, and weights in grams and kilograms.

Health Precautions

The biggest risk to your health is the strong summer sun. If you are visiting in summer be sure to pack sunscreen, light clothing that allows your skin to breathe and a hat. Dehydration can also be a problem, so it is important to drink lots of water. Tap water is safe to drink everywhere. Those spending prolonged periods in Croatia's mountains and forests should consider vaccinating against tick-borne encephalitis – a potentially fatal viral infection that can cause swelling on and around the brain and spinal cord. Frequent travellers should already be vaccinated against Hepatitis A. Although rare, there have been reported cases of rabies in Croatia. To protect yourself against this disease do not pet stray animals and seek medical advice immediately if one bites you. Planning ahead can also help keep you healthy when you are travelling, like ensuring that you have enough of your prescribed medicines or contact lenses and even having a dental check up before you leave home. Precautions should also be taken against sexually transmitted diseases.

Health Services

There is a hospital or medical centre in all the main towns. Dialling **94** will call out an emergency ambulance. Hospitals and pharmacies are well equipped and stocked.

Personal Safety

Croatia is a relatively safe country to visit, with comparatively low crime rates, particularly outside of its cities. Tourists rarely fall victim to serious crime, but petty thefts do occur. If a crime is committed against you report it to the police immediately, particularly if you plan on claiming from your insurance company. Croatians are used to females travelling alone so this should not cause you any problems.

Emergencies

In an emergency call:
Police: 92
Fire Brigade: 93
Ambulance: 94
Emergency road service: 987
Coast guard: 985

Etiquette

Croatian's consider it polite to greet one another before starting a conversation. A simple *Dobro Jutro* (good morning) or *Dobar Dan* (good day) will set you in good stead.

Language

Croatian uses Roman script, although it has five extra letters: č, ć, ž, š and đ, as well as a variety of different sounds. A good phrase book is recommended.

Public Holidays

1 January **New Year's Day**
6 January **Epiphany/Three Kings' Day**
March/April **Good Friday**
March/April **Easter Monday**
1 May **Labour Day**
30 May **Corpus Christi**
22 June **Anti-Fascist Day**
25 June **Croatian National Day**
5 August **Victory Day/ National Thanksgiving Day**
15 August **Feast of the Assumption**
8 October **Independence Day**
1 November **All Saints' Day**
25–26 December **Christmas Holidays**

Festivals

• **Carnival, Rijeka** (Feb) Carnival parades, theatrical performances, exhibitions and comedy shows.
• **Dubrovnik Summer Festival** (Jul–Aug) The walled city comes alive with music, theatre and street entertainment during this renowned annual festival that spans six weeks. Venues that are normally closed to the public open up their doors for performances.
• **Zagreb Summer Festival** (Jun/Jul) Enjoy contemporary and traditional music and theatre in the capital.
• **The International Children's Festival, Šibenik** (Jun/Jul) A ten-day celebration of children's theatre and art.
• **The Summer of Split** (Jul/Aug) Another of Dalmatia's summer festivals sees outdoor stages throughout the city fill with theatrical performances, classical music, ballet, opera and pop concerts.

GOOD READING

Tanner, Marcus (2001) *Croatia: A Nation Forged in War.* Yale University Press, New Haven and London
Slavenka Drakulić (1993) *Balkan Express: Fragments from the Other Side of War.* Hutchinson, London. Random House, Australia, New Zealand and South Africa.
Ugrešić, Dubravka (1998) *The Culture of Lies (Translated by Celia Hawkesworth).* Weidenfeld and Nicholson, London.
Mešic, Stipe (2004) *The Demise of Yugoslavia: A Political Memoir.* Central European University Press, New York.

• **Musical Evenings in St Donat's Church, Zadar** (Jul/Aug) Enchanting classical music fills the interior of this historic church.
• **Pula Film Festival** (Jul/Aug) Catch the latest international and domestic screen offerings in the city's atmospheric Roman Amphitheatre.
• **Vinkovci Autumn Festival** (Sep) An annual two-day event celebrating centuries of Croatian folklore.
• **Varaždin Baroque Evenings** (20 Sep to 6 Oct) A fortnight of opera and baroque performances, by companies from all over Croatia, in Varaždin.
• **World Music Festival - Nebo, Zagreb** (Ocy/Nov) Four-day festival showcasing traditional, folk, ethnic and contemporary music from performers across the world.

INDEX

Note: Numbers in **bold** indicate photographs